TONY SWAIN

NARRATIVE DEFICIENCIES THROUGHOUT

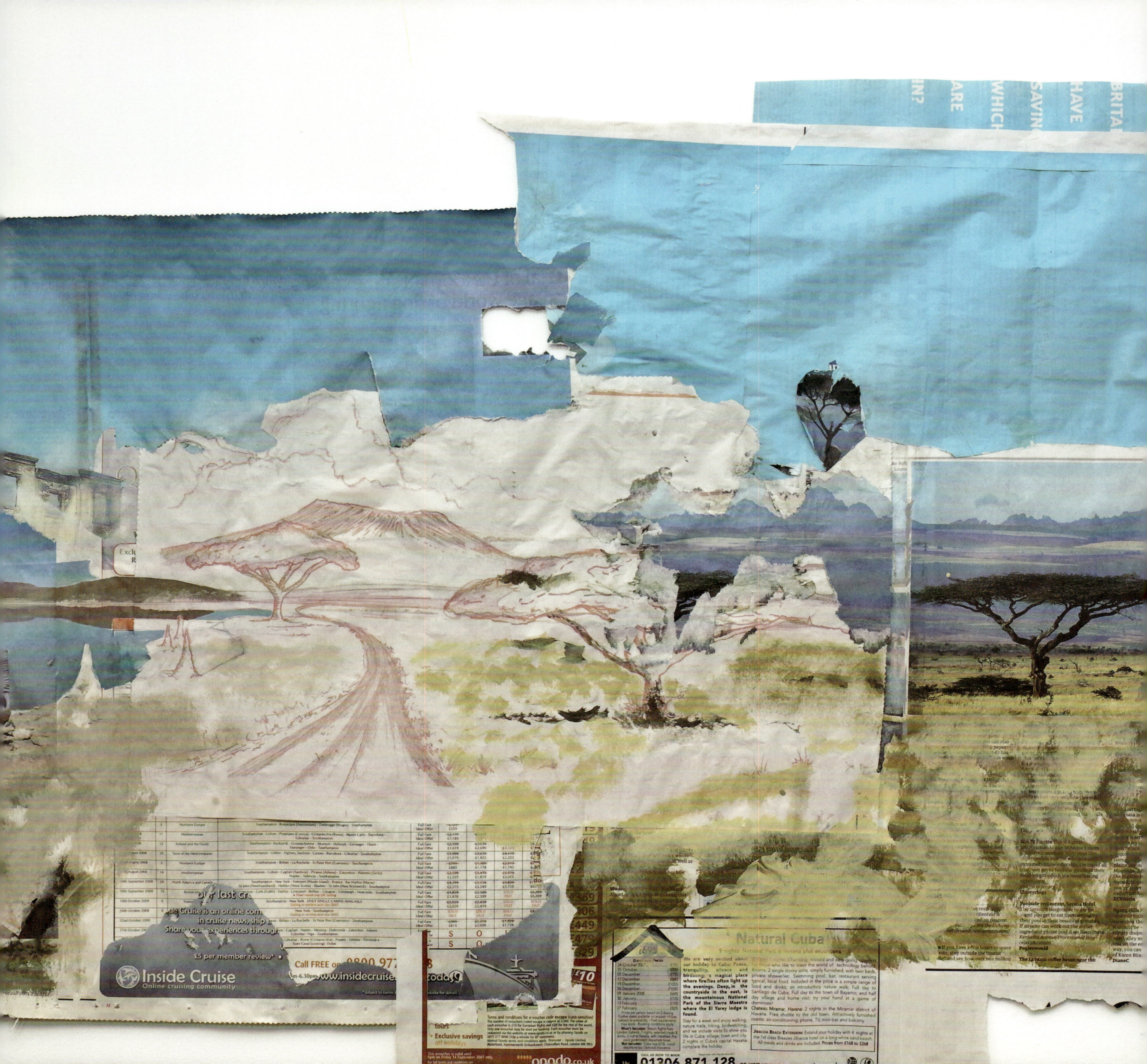

Inside Cruise
Online cruising community
...de Cruise is an online com...
in cruise news, ship...
Share your experiences through...
£5 per member review*
Call FREE on 0800 977...
www.insidecruise...
opodo
Exclusive savings
off holidays
Natural Cuba
We are very excited about our holiday to Cuba. Peace, tranquillity, silence and birdsong; a magical place where fireflies often light up the evenings. Deep, in the countryside in the east, is the mountainous National Park of the Sierra Maestra where the El Yarey lodge is found.
Stay for a week and enjoy walking, nature trails, hiking, birdwatching, and we include visits to show you life in Cuba: village, town and city. 2 nights in Cuba's capital Havana complete the holiday.
Chateau Miramar, Havana 2 nights in the Miramar district of Havana. Free shuttle to the old town. Attractively furnished rooms: air-conditioning, phone, TV, mini-bar and balcony.
JIBACOA BEACH EXTENSION: Extend your holiday with 4 nights at the 1st class Breezes Jibacoa hotel on a long white sand beach. All meals and drinks are included. Prices from £168 to £268
CALL US NOW TO BOOK
01306 871 128

TONY SWAIN

NARRATIVE DEFICIENCIES THROUGHOUT

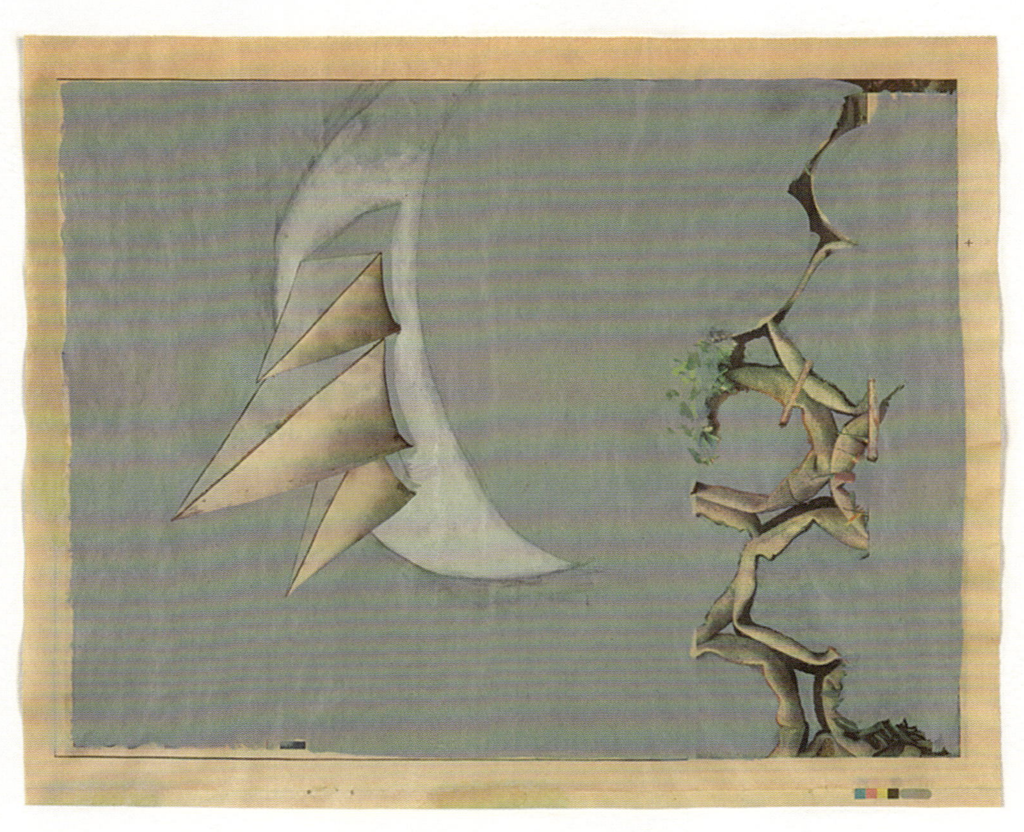

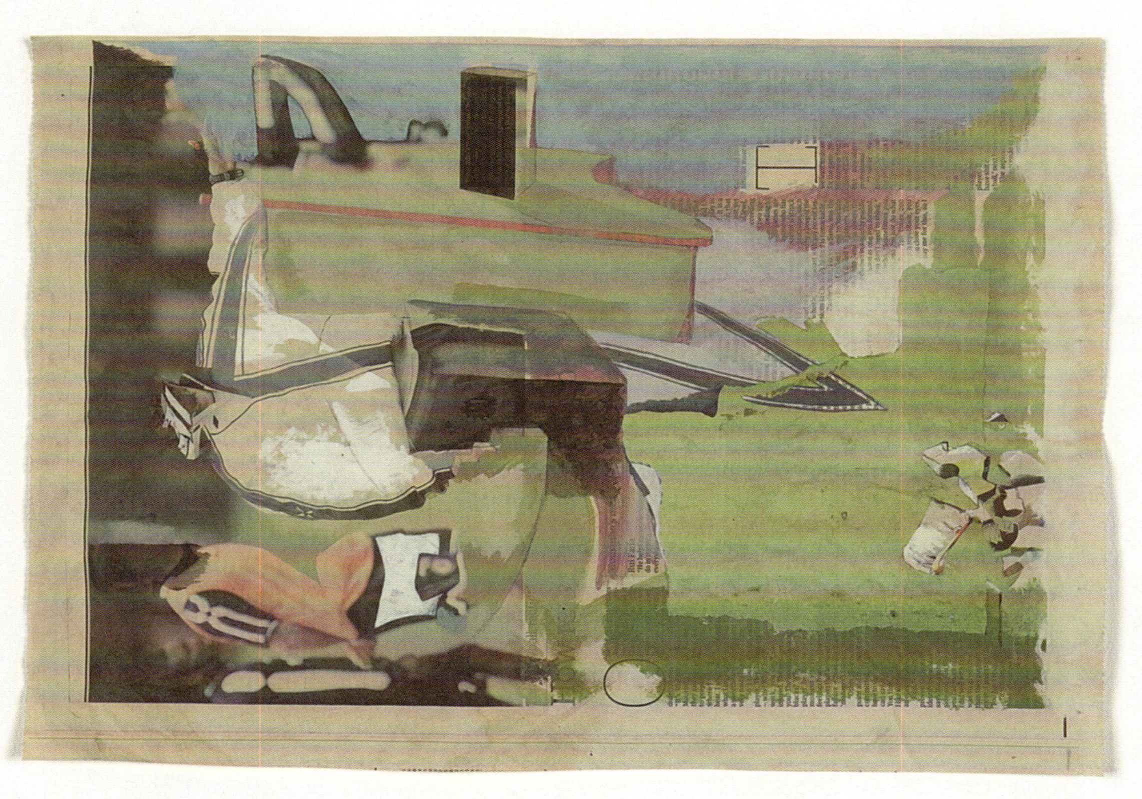

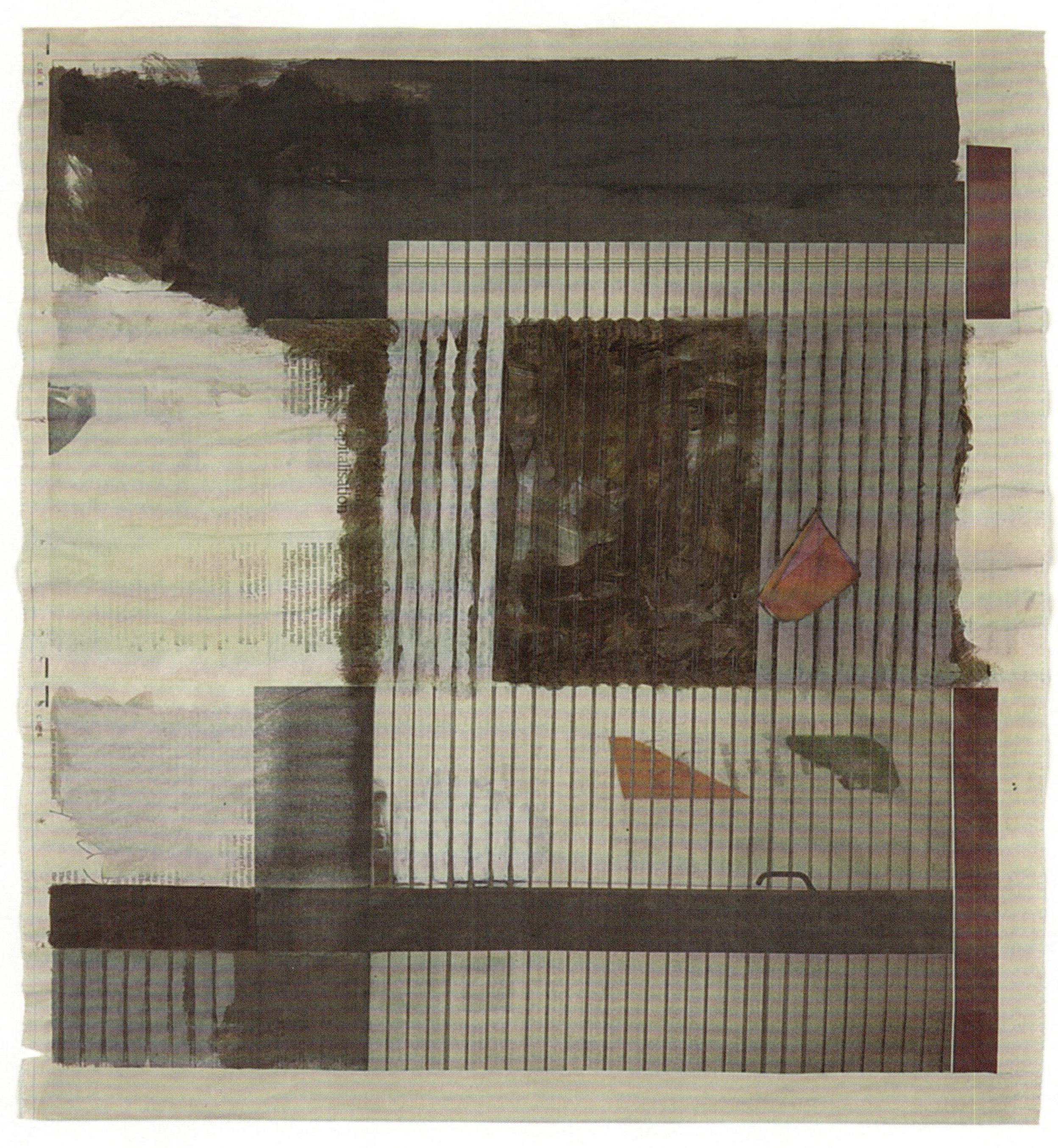

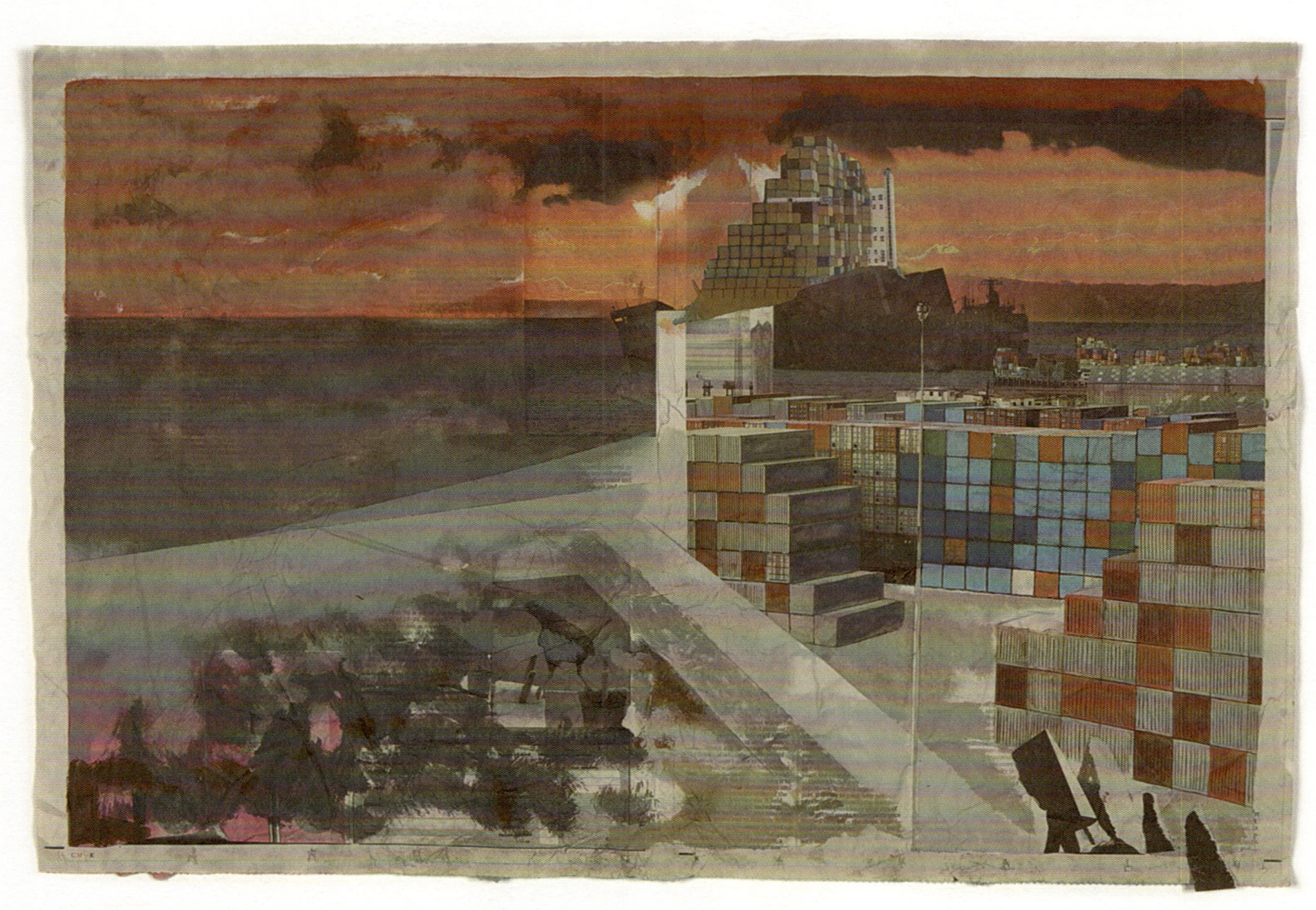

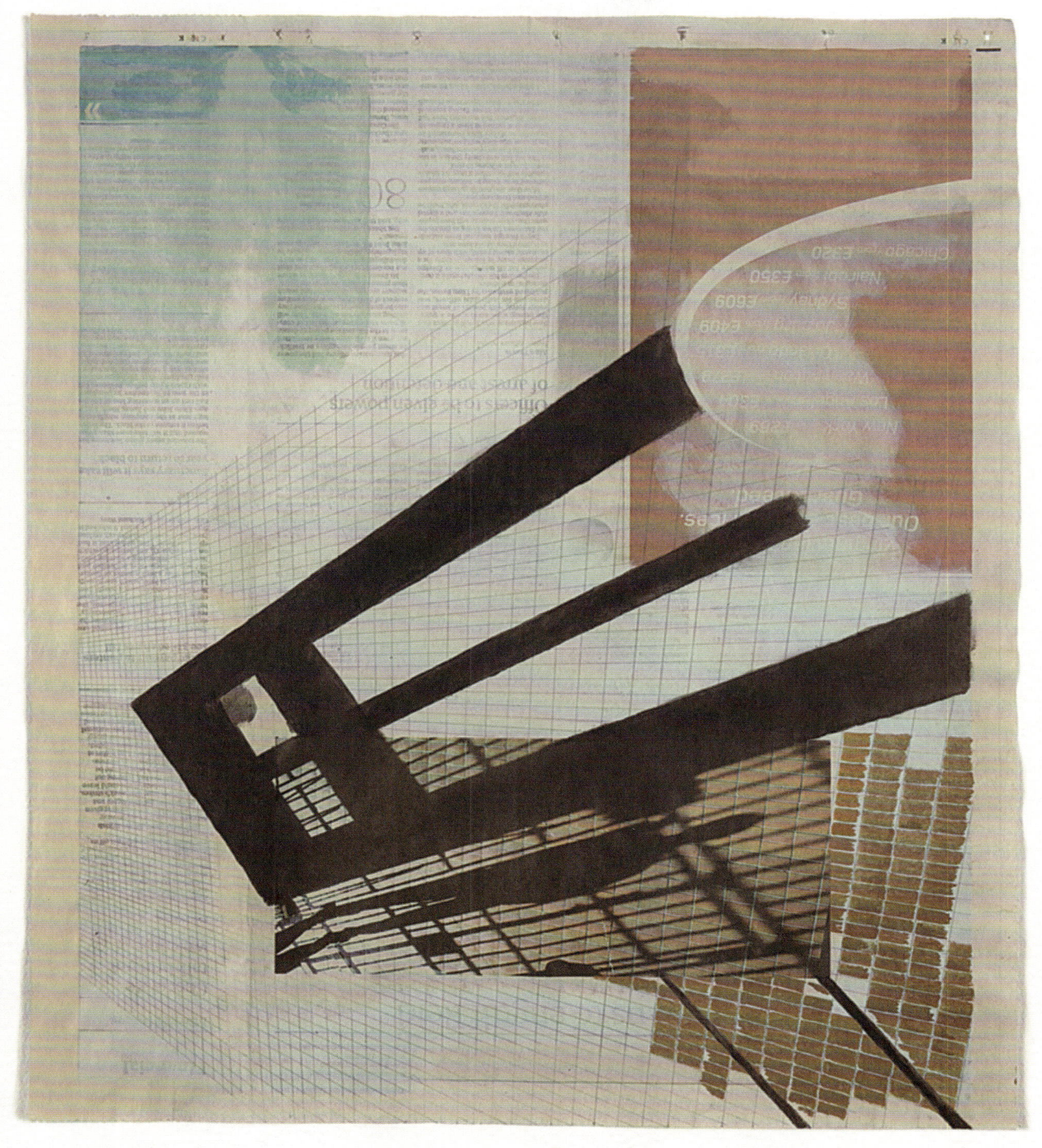

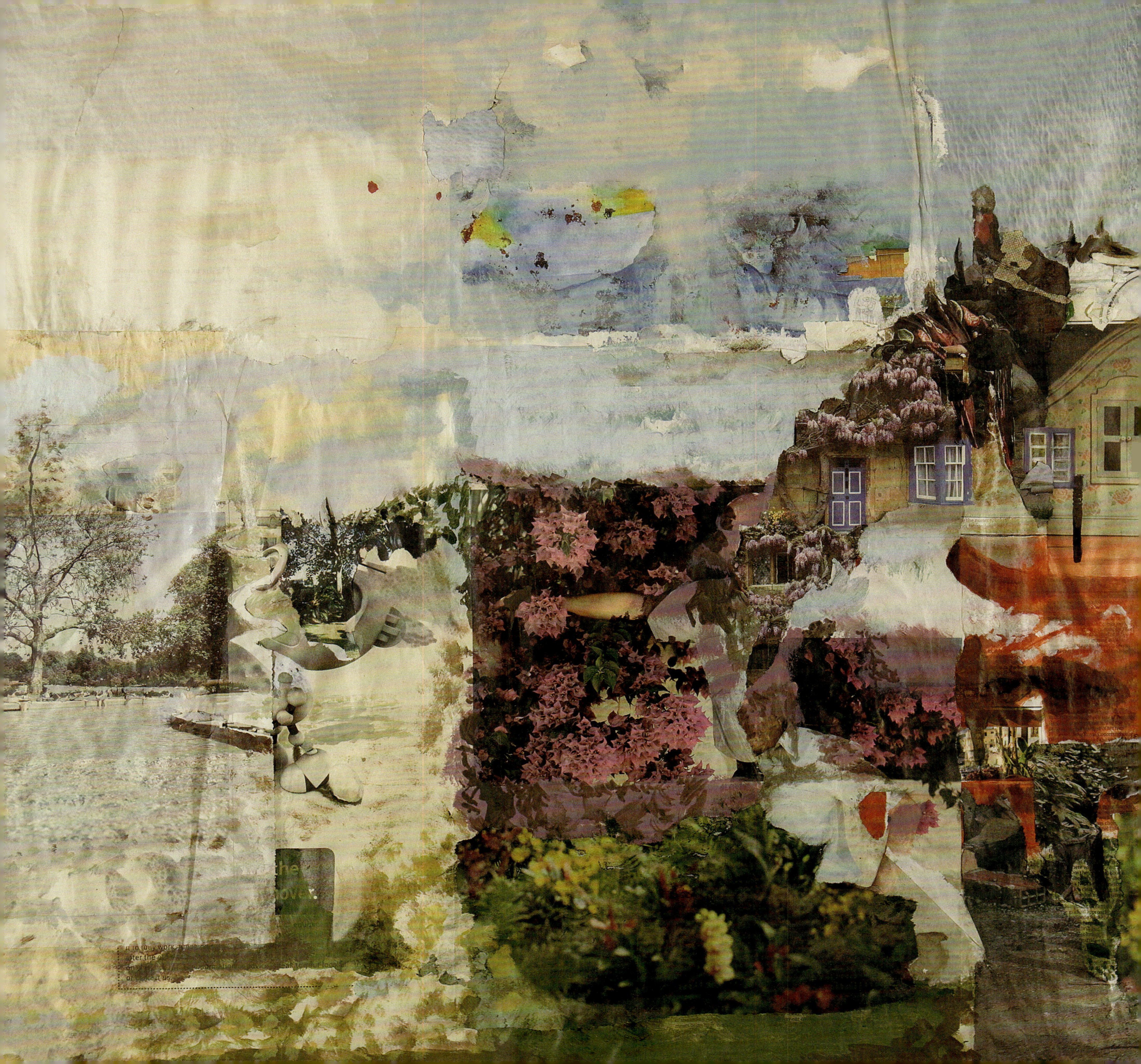

INTRODUCTION

Fiona Bradley

Tony Swain paints landscapes, cityscapes, seascapes
and interiors, frequented and constructed by mountains,
sand dunes, meadows, trees, rocks, lighthouses, power
stations, landmarks both natural and man-made,
boats, bridges, buildings, houses, furniture and
domestic objects. His imagery is often on a vast
scale, encompassing huge vistas, but also collapses
into intimacy. The marks he makes most usually
organise themselves into representation, but sometimes
remain as passages of painterly abstraction. A lot
of the work generates the expectation of narrative,
seeming to lead somewhere both conceptually and
formally, yet it eschews this expectation, working
instead on and with the picture plane. The large
painting *Jesus Help Me Find My Property* (2007;
pp.32–33) offers many potential routes along its
three metre length. Yet these are not set up by the
painting's provocative title, but rather by its formal
pictorial tropes – the boats, the jetty, the sweeping
path to the volcano, the chapel on the hill. So too the
marks and rips of *The Tribute to Inquiry* (2010; p.87)
or *Coping and more than coping* (2011; p.92) which,
for all the connotations of these titles, keep the viewer
firmly in the moment in which they are encountered.

Swain's work speaks to a number of different traditions,
and its radicality – and the starting point for most
commentators and viewers – lies not in what it is
of but what it is on. Painting on newspaper adds
a particular dimension to the paintings, at once
comforting and disconcerting. The artist himself
is not that interested in his support per se – it is just
what he reaches for when he wants to start painting.
The choice of it does play a part in the development
of his practice, though, having helped him out of an
impasse which stopped him painting for several years.
Now, it is part of his routine. His day starts, as does
many people's, with a read of the paper. As he reads,
he scans for things he can use, moving between
reading and looking. Things he can use trigger
a sense of recognition, almost as if they look like the
beginnings of a painting. It's a subversive process,
using the imagery chosen by the paper's picture editor
for the artist's own ends, but the subversion does not
have a particular target. His practice is political, but
not in the way you might expect art made with
newspaper to be: when he paints out the head of
a politician it is primarily because it is in the way.

Newspaper has an important place in the history
of art, most notably in the context of dada and surrealist
collage. An agent of disjunction and disruption, dada
collage valued fragmentation, transformation and
the frustration of expectation above almost everything.
It attacked the established hierarchies of images and

the media from which art was made. In surrealism,
collage served to shift the initial agency of the art image
away from its author, valuing it as a chance procedure
that might give rise to the kind of unexpected
juxtapositions commonly found in dreams. Swain
is interested in newspaper's history in art, though
his work does not always look like collage, and is often
not really collage at all. When he sticks sections of
newspaper together it is to extend the picture plane
rather than to disrupt it, and his paintings, even the
most abstract, are characterised by a search for visual
coherence rather than breakdown. Swain's admiration
for the collages of dadaist Kurt Schwitters has to do
with the artist's ability to make lasting imagery out
of the detritus of everyday life. This is something
Swain has in common with Schwitters, and to me
is related more to the basic alchemy of art – the
capacity to make something meaningful out of not
very much – than to collage.

Swain's reading and reworking of the newspaper
provides him with both an armature on which to
hang a painting and some constraints within and
with which to work. Moving out from the image
which first attracted him, he paints or covers over
with other found images the remains of the page,
building a composition which follows the logic of
representational painting. Thus *Too-valued blue*
(2007; p.25) and *Untitled* (2010; p.79). The first
a landscape, the second a seascape, both paintings

use the repetition of an image found in the paper
(a tree, a lighthouse) as their inspiration and
organising principle. Looking at them now, it is
hard to tell where they started – Swain's processes
are not easily unpicked – and even what has been
altered and how. Is it the same photograph of the
same lighthouse? Different photographs of the same
lighthouse? Different lighthouses? And are the trees
all the same? Both lighthouse and tree lead the eye
across and into the paintings, whose lyrical yet somehow
urgent beauty precludes the looking becoming too
much of a guessing game. After a while, it matters
not at all what the paintings started with, or what
is found and what is made, photograph or painting.
The works work as a whole, completely compelling.

The painting *Persistence is* (2010; p.104) moves the
eye across and into its surface, the repeated horizontals
slanting from bottom left to top right, tracking yet
subverting the way the surface might be read if it were
still a page. Roads, paths, railings and stretches of sea
are classic Swain tropes, precisely because they conjure
space from nowhere, transforming page into painting.
In this work, representation, both painted and printed,
is balanced by abstraction, also both painted and printed
– the ghostly old pier in the top left quarter of the
painting is answered in the bottom right by a wonderful
sequence of loosely painted muted pink and blue marks
which bracket and direct a pale green printed border.
As with so much of Swain's work, the painting moves
effortlessly between dimensions, one minute asking
you to look at it, the next pulling you through.

This book reproduces around 65 paintings. It brings
together works made between 2006 and 2012 and
picks up from where *Paintings*, a monograph published
by DuMont in 2008, leaves off. It is published to
accompany a solo exhibition of new work at The
Fruitmarket Gallery in Edinburgh, and includes some
of the work which will be presented in that exhibition.
We are grateful to Tony Swain for working with us
to produce the publication, and for making new work
for the exhibition. We are delighted to be able to share
his work with our audience, and to have the opportunity
to commission a new essay from Isla Leaver-Yap
with which to contextualise and assess his practice,

and a conversation between Tony Swain and artist
Karla Black. Artists ask each other different questions
from those a curator or writer might ask, and this
is a particularly generous and enlightening exchange.

Tony Swain's preferred method in making solo
exhibitions is to show only work made in the
period since his previous exhibition, so there
is a different rhythm and sense of time passing
in the publication than there will be in the exhibition.
This seems to complement the sense of time
in the work – the paintings, made on something
so absolutely concerned with the marking of time,
are both in time and also out of it.

____

*Fiona Bradley is Director of The Fruitmarket Gallery,
Edinburgh*

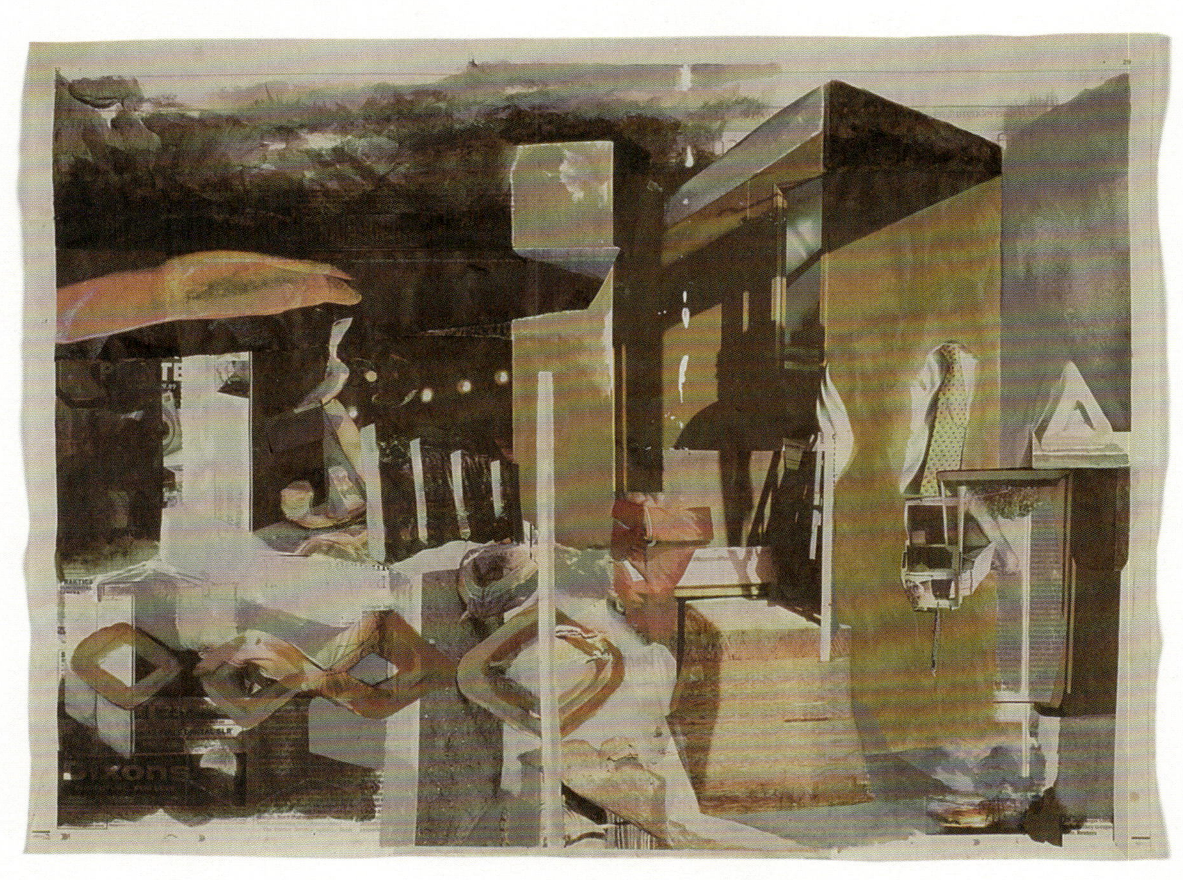

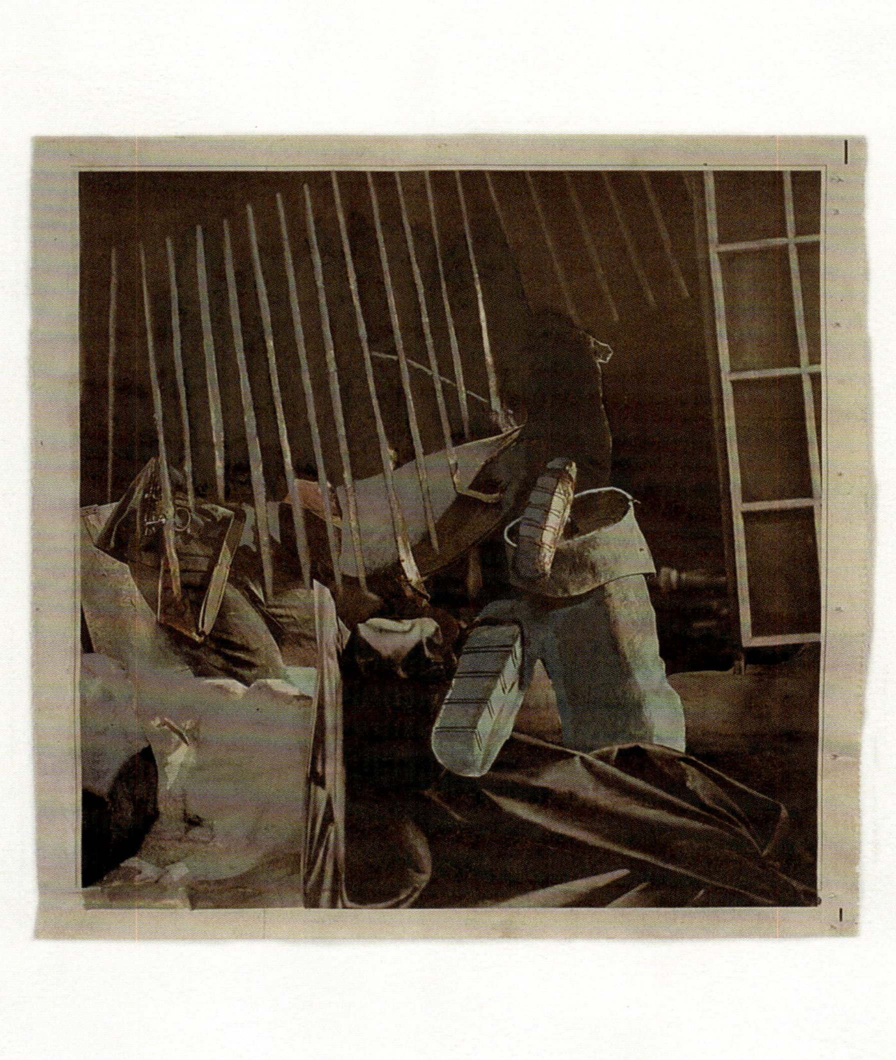

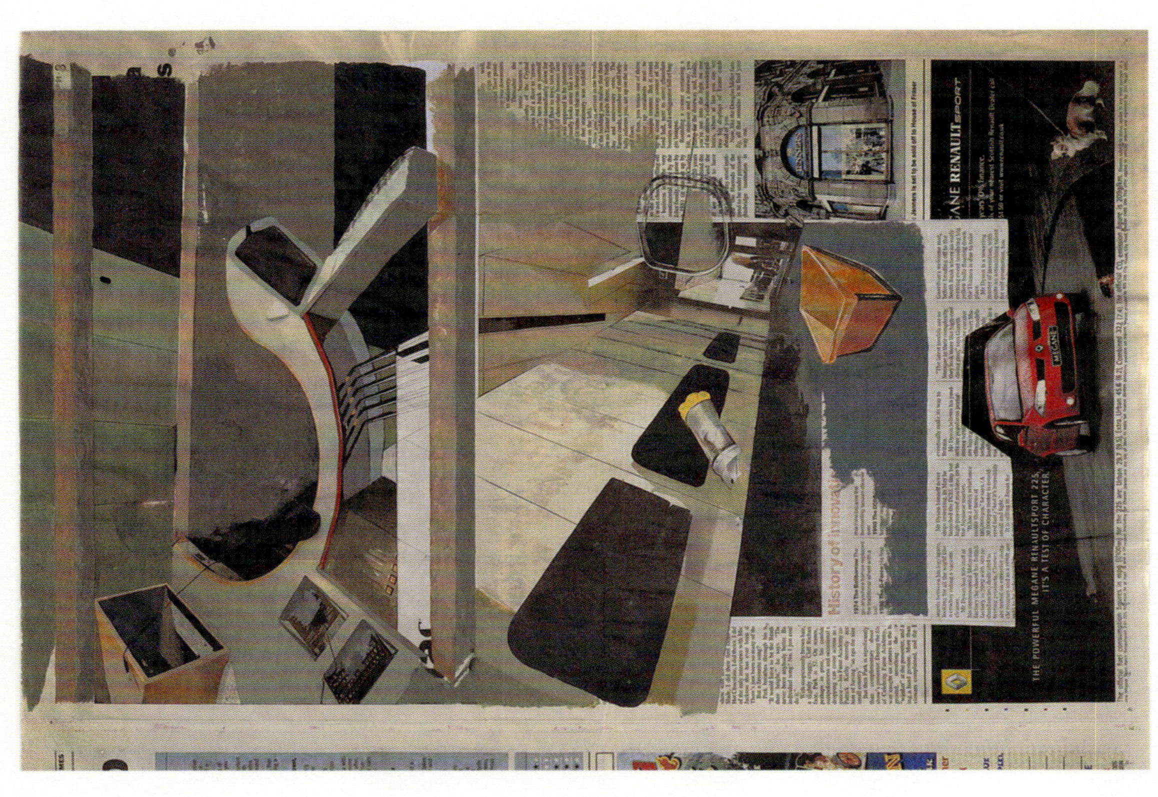

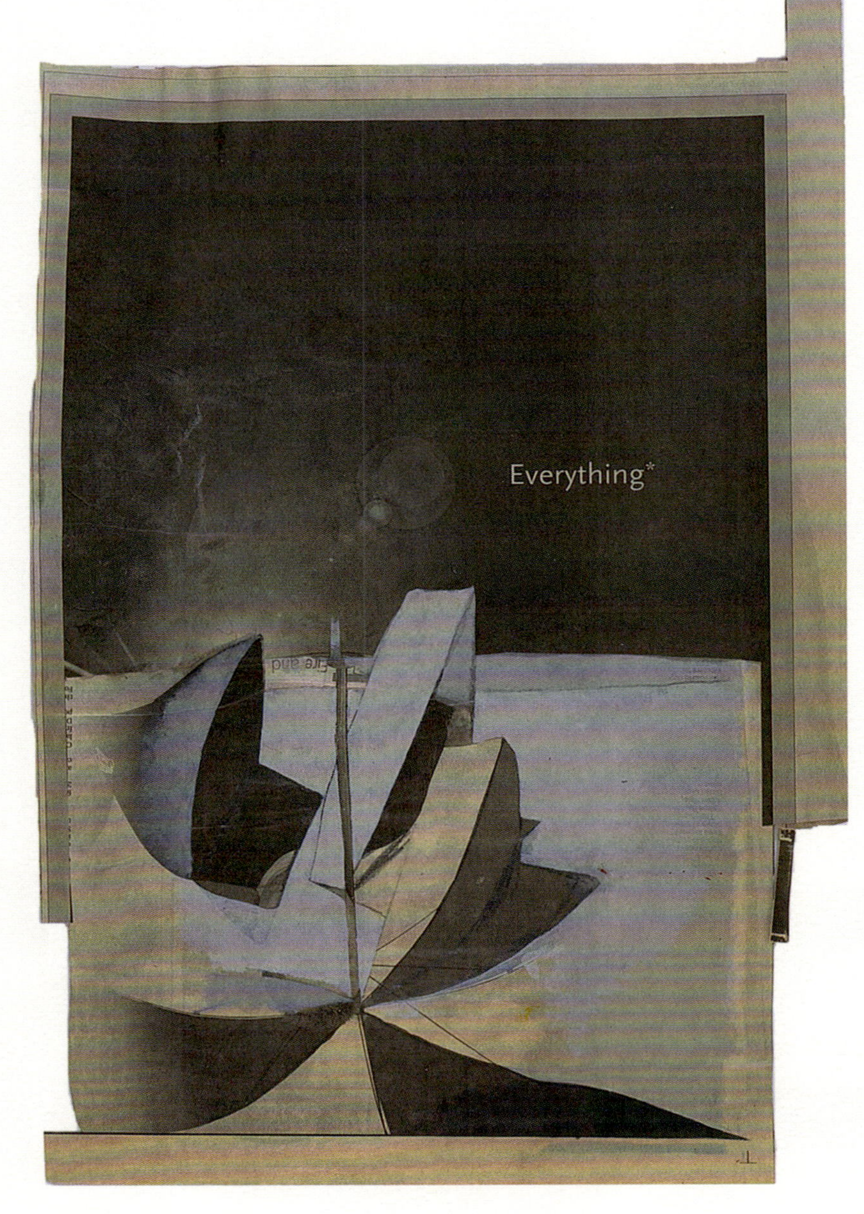
Everything*

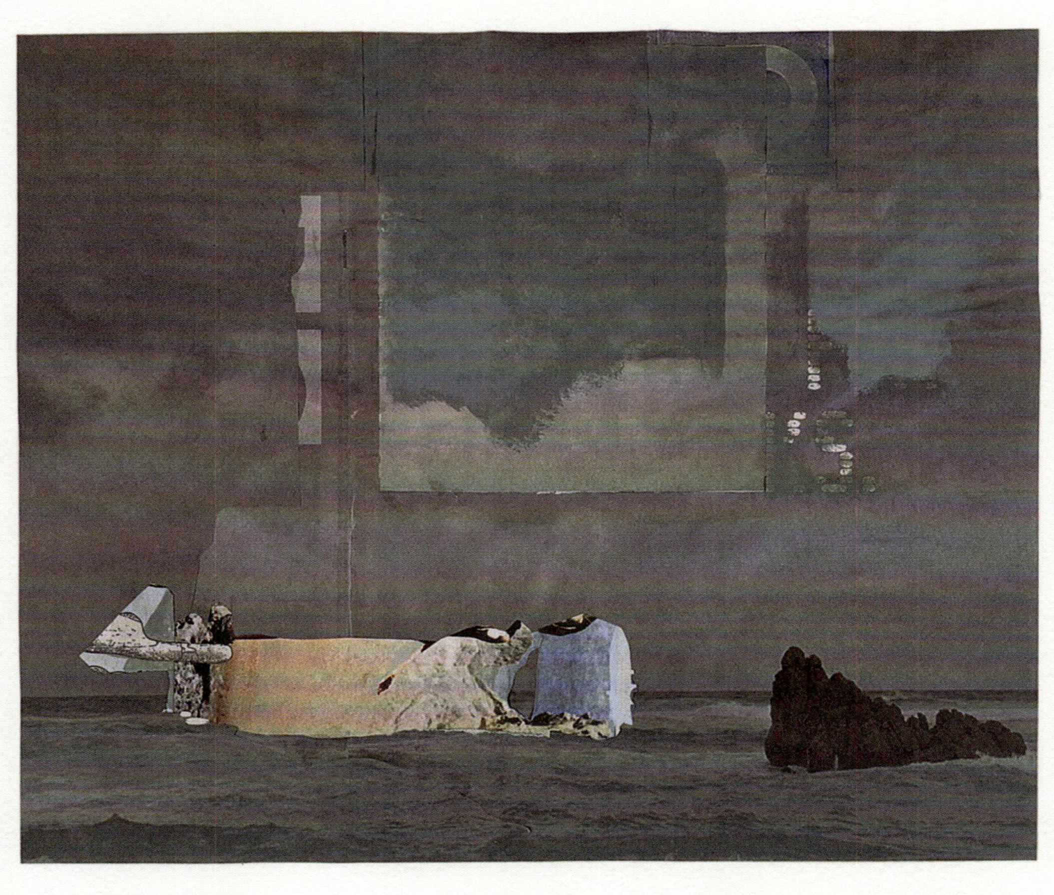

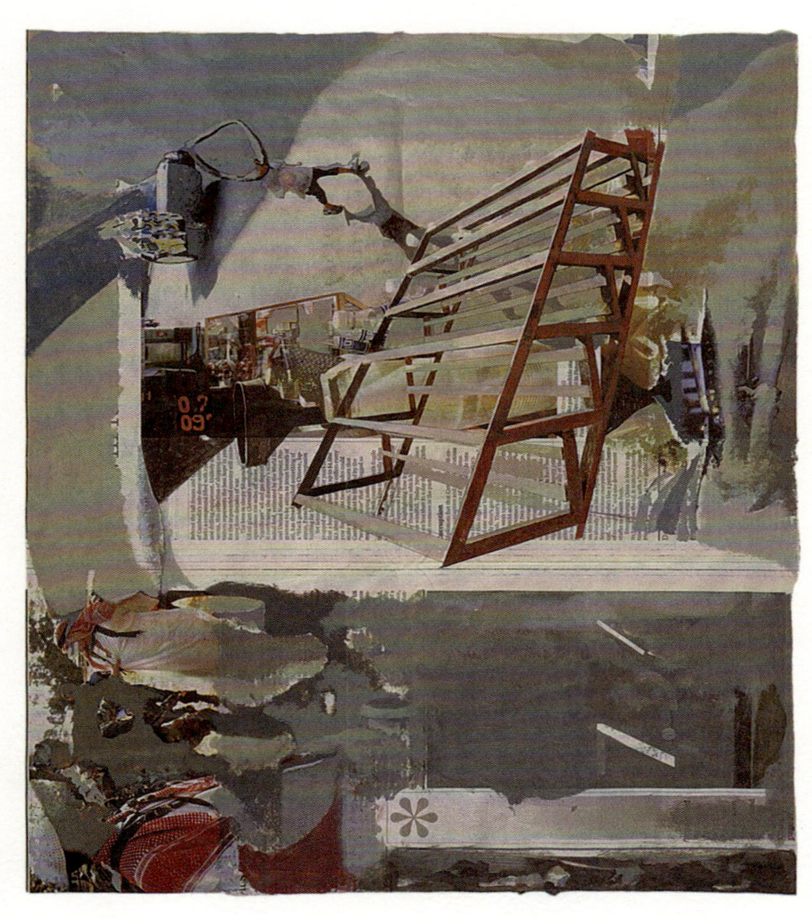

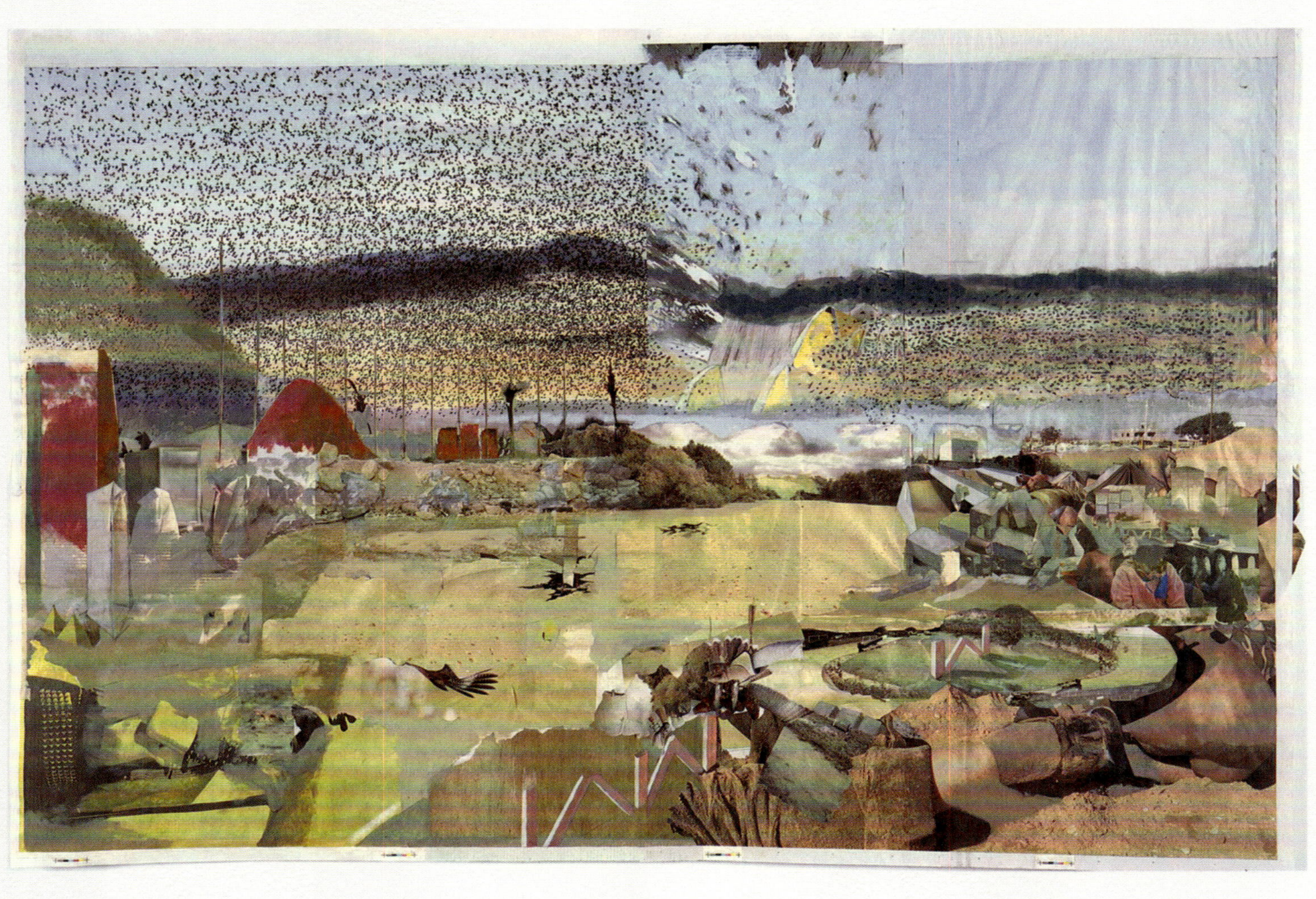

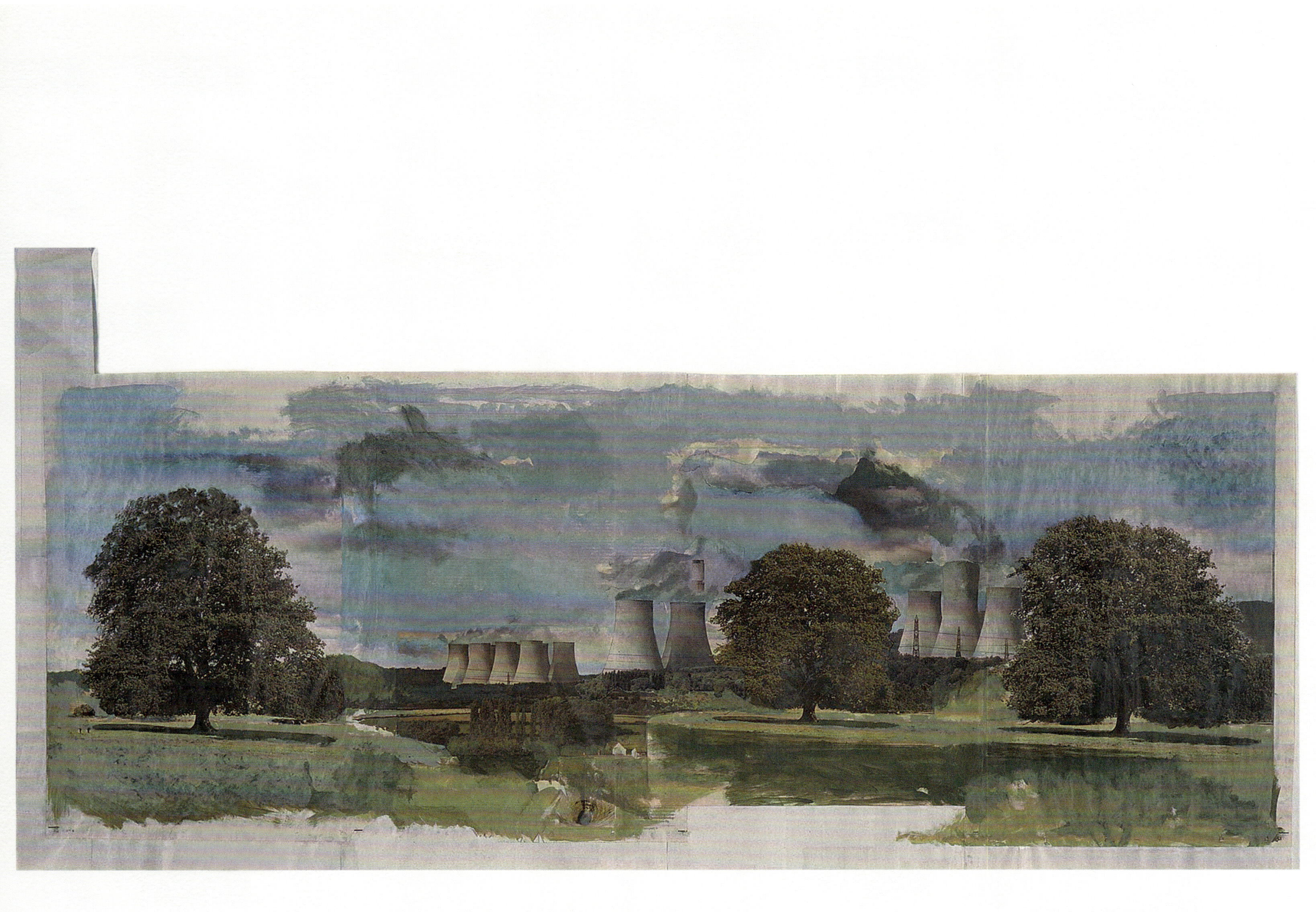

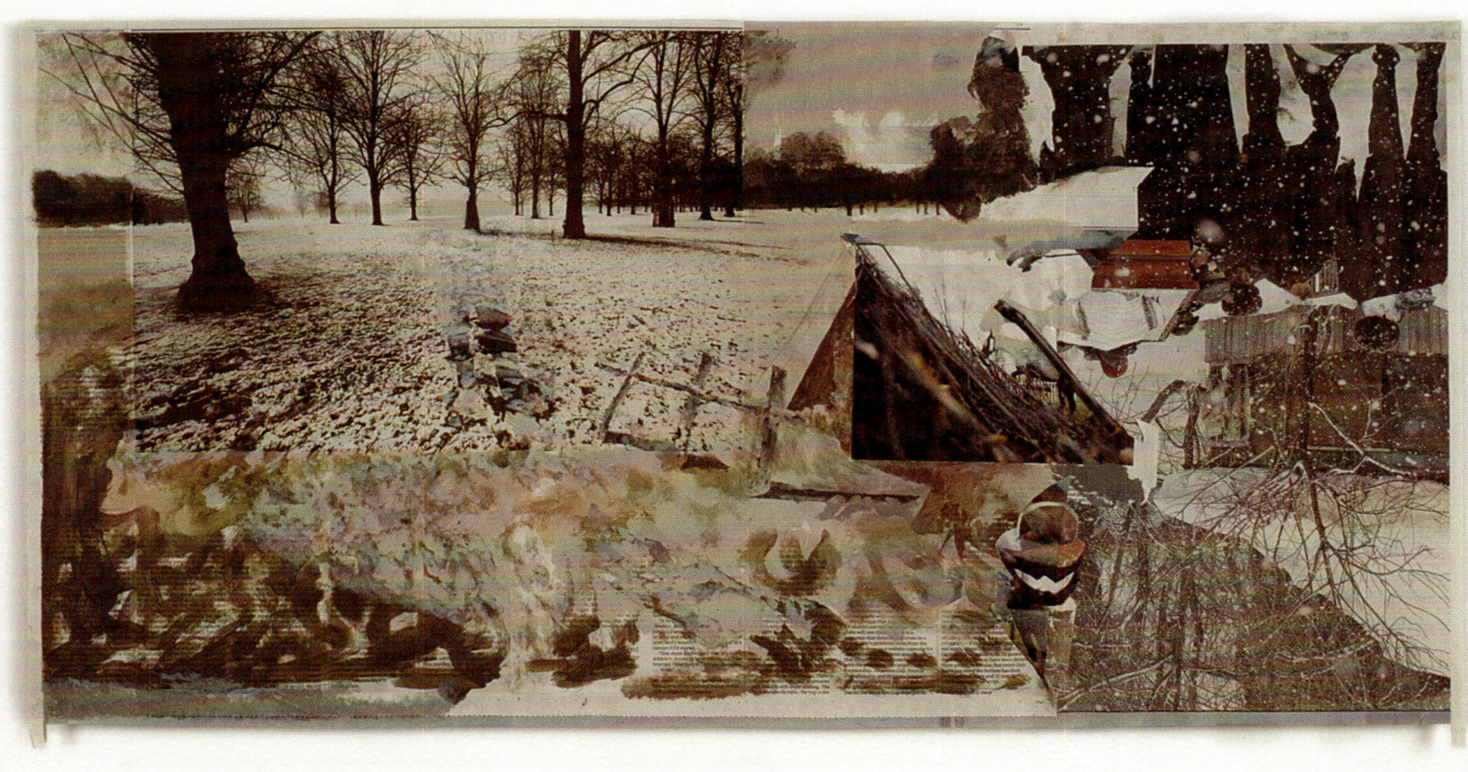

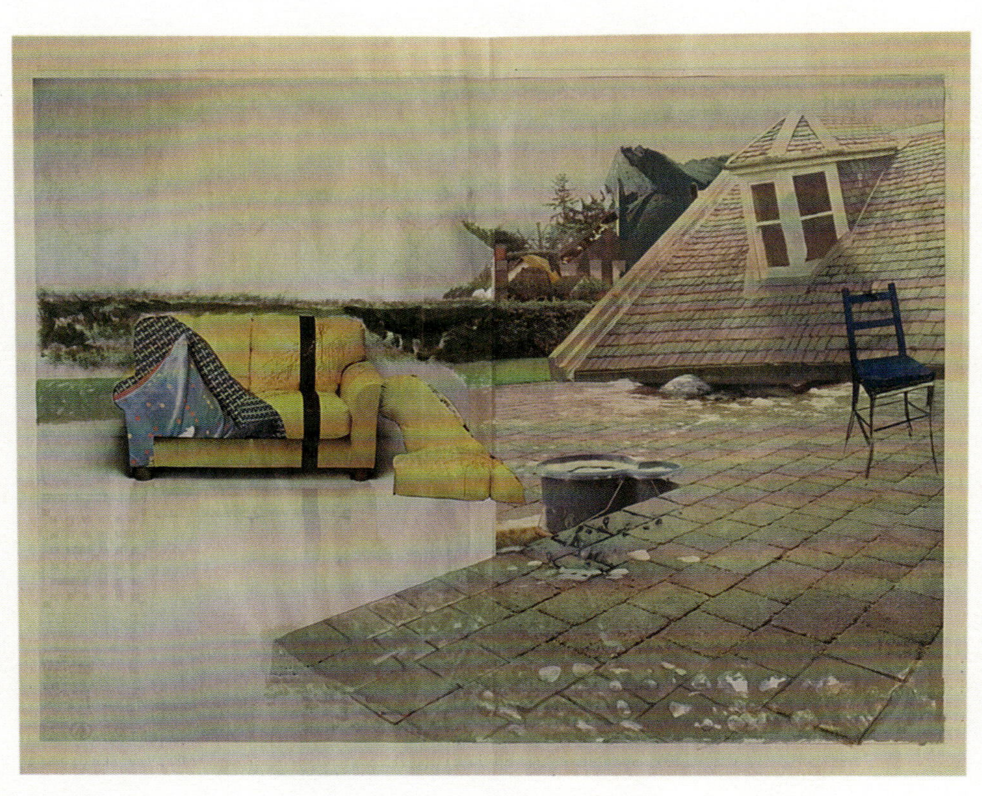

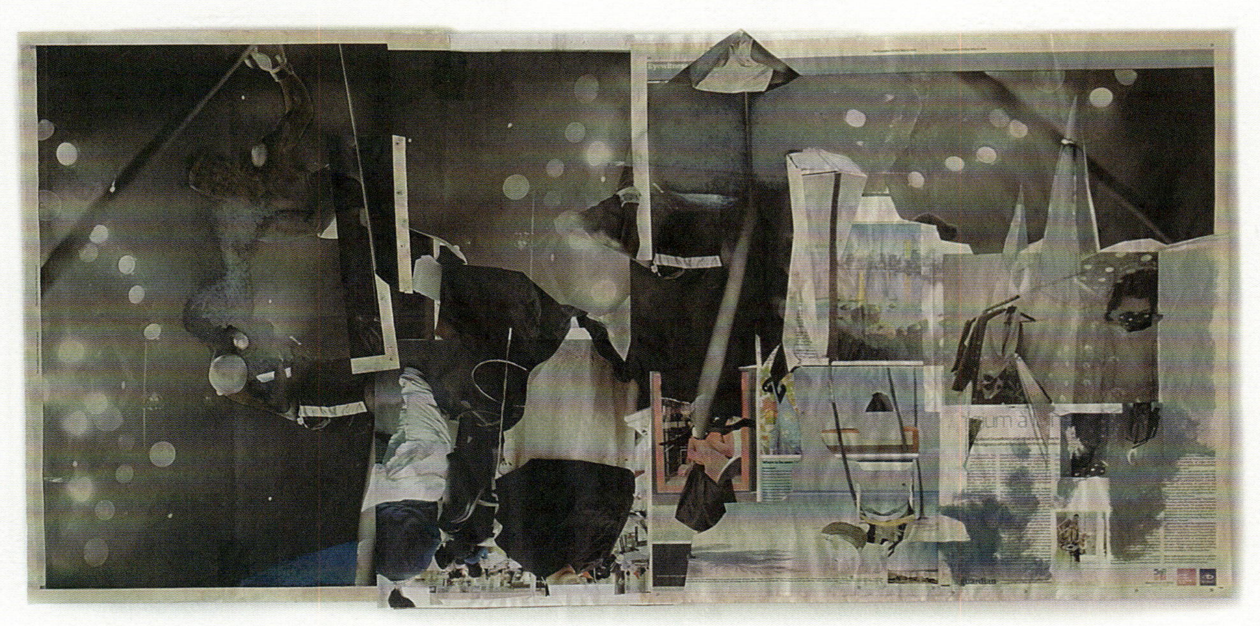

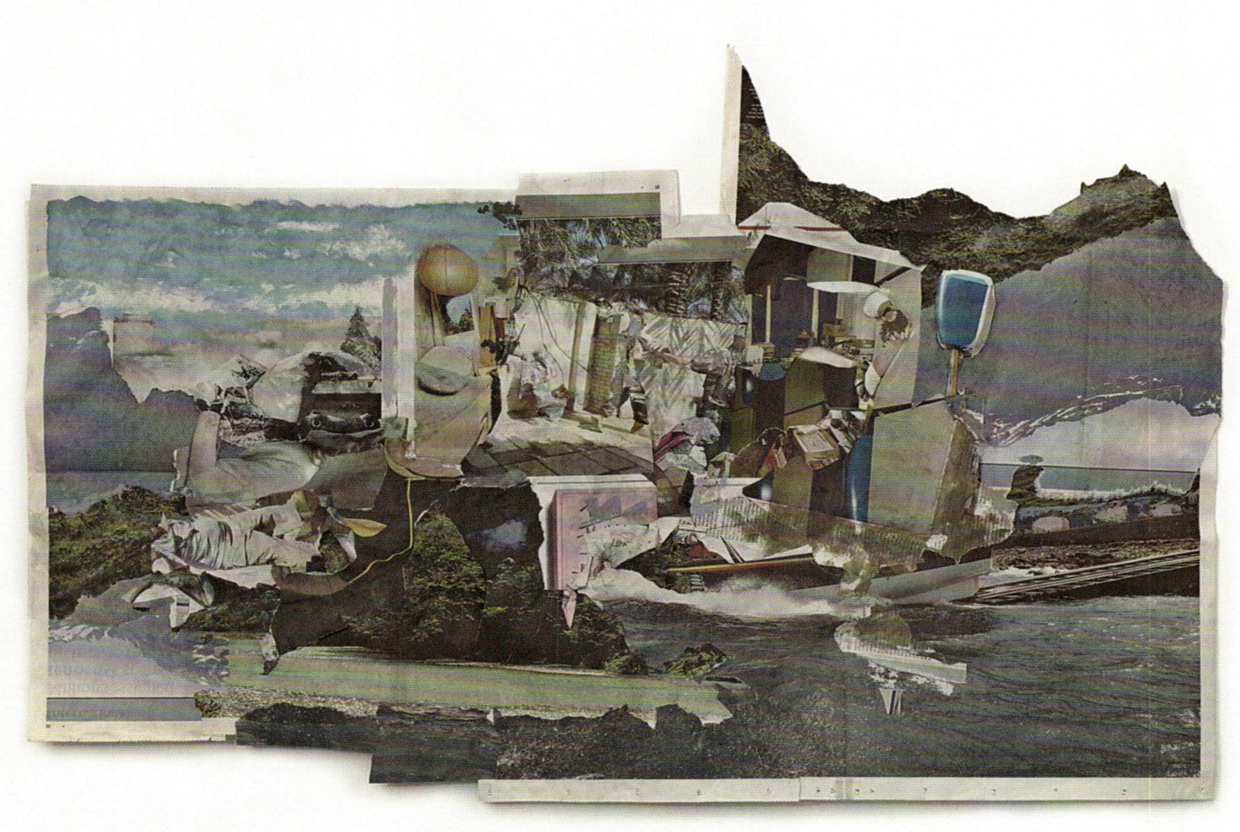

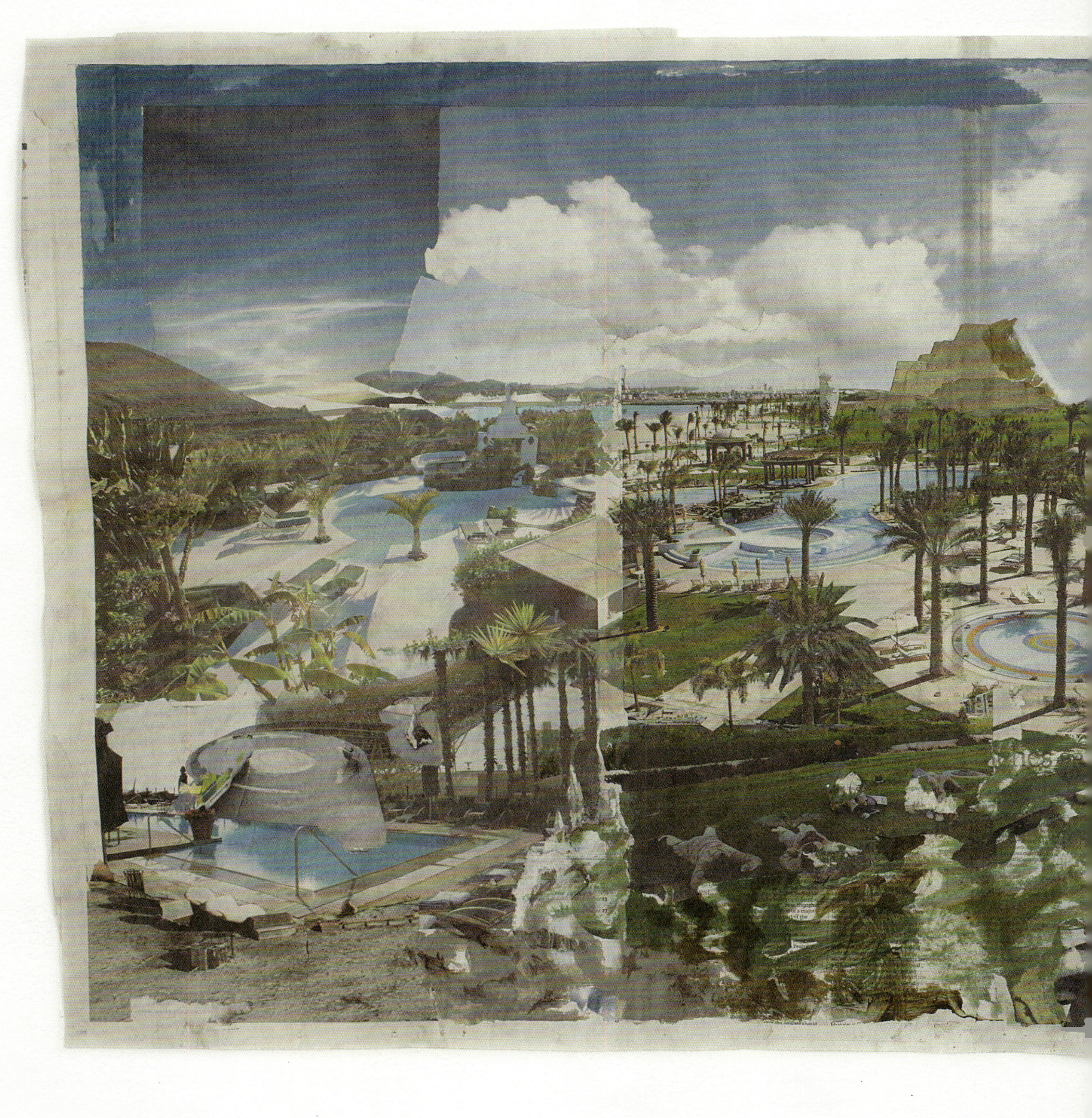

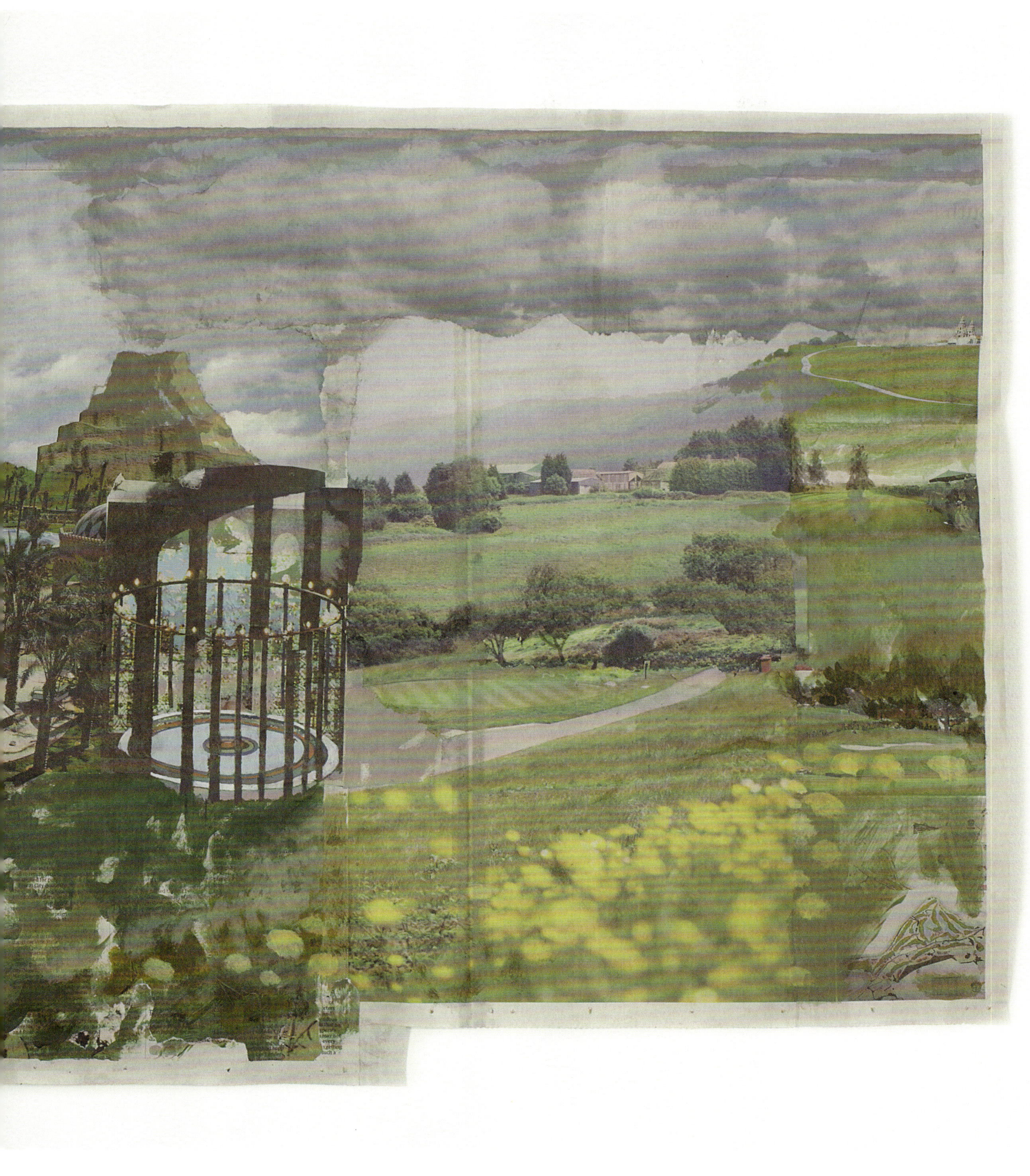

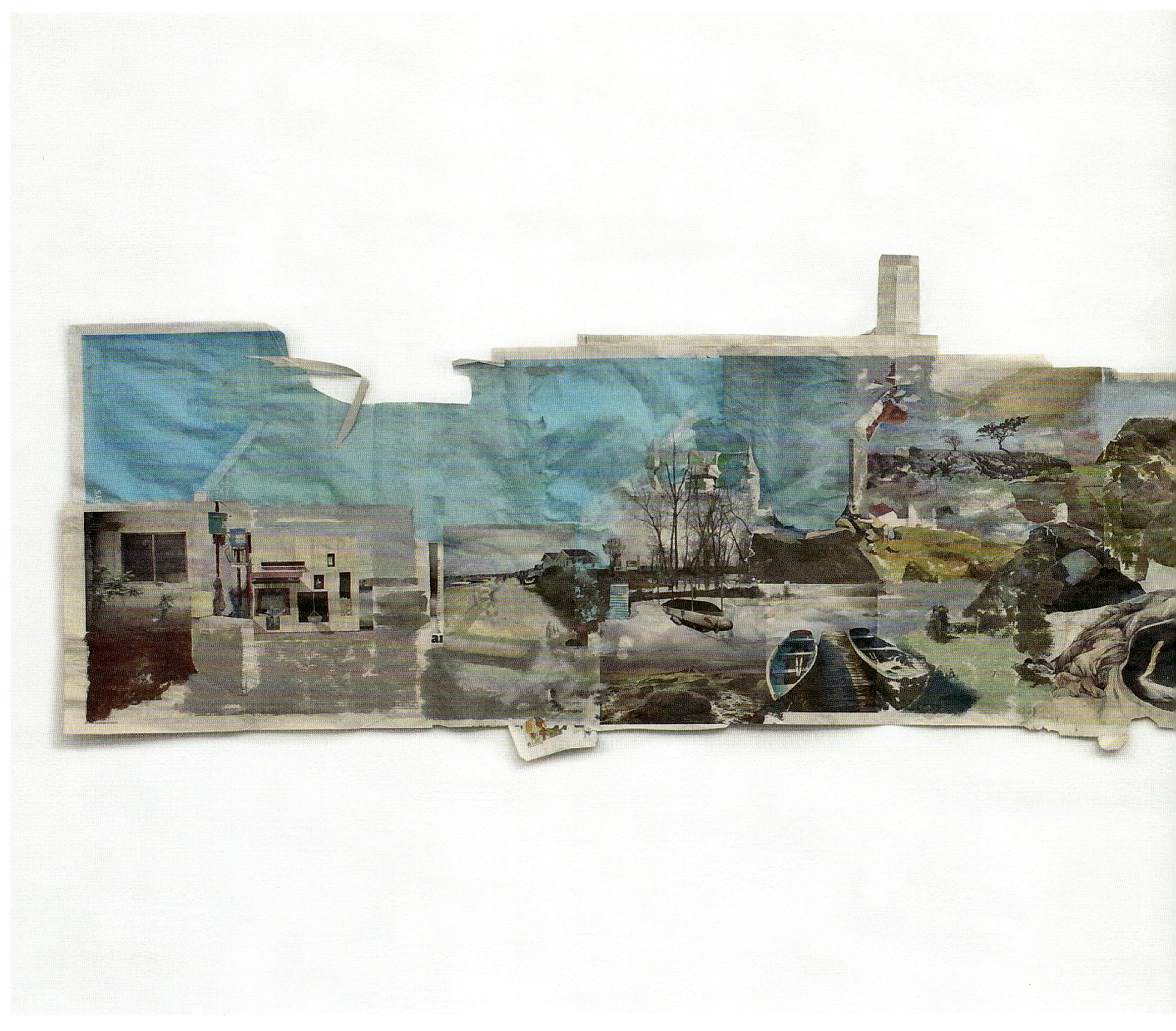

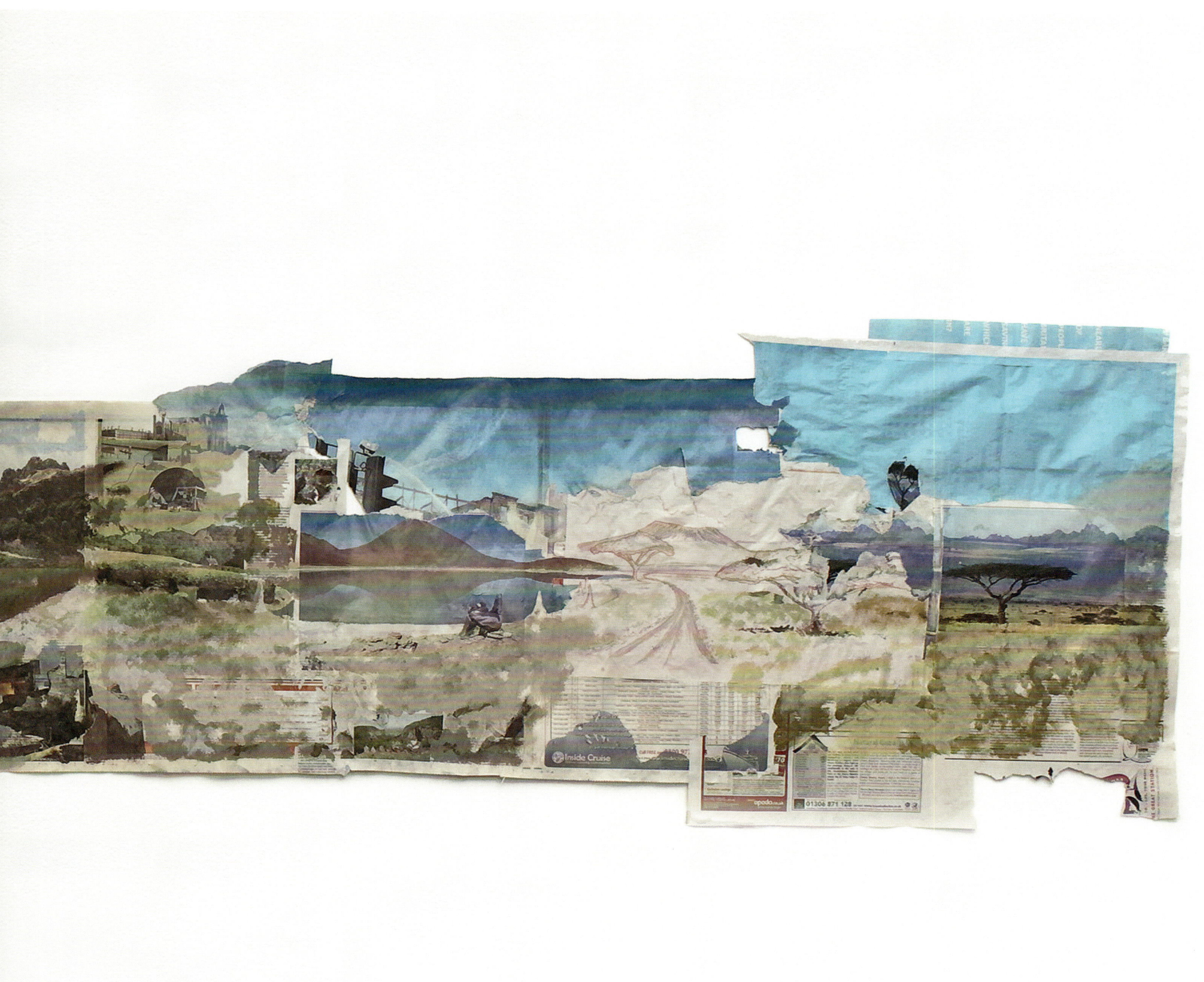

Inside Cruise
Call FREE on 0800 977
apodo.co.uk
01306 871 128
THE GREAT STATION

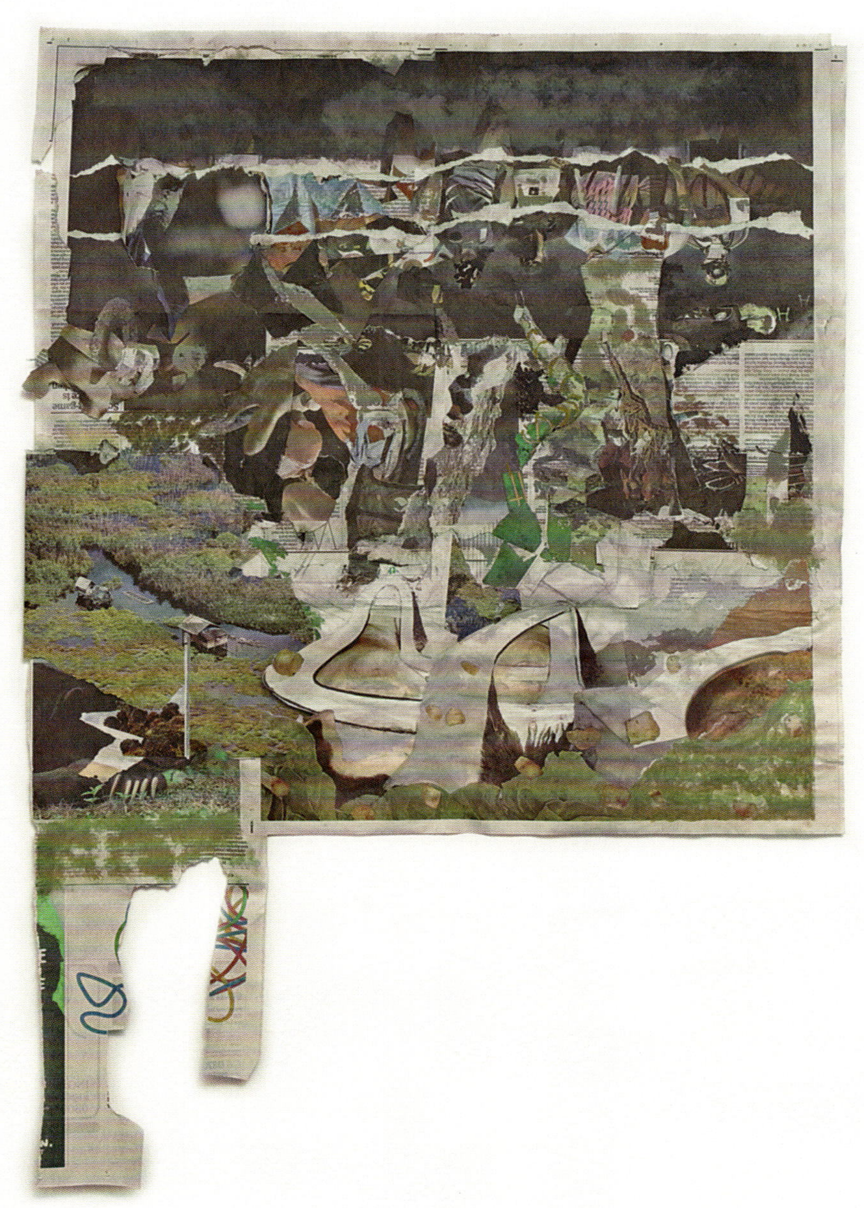

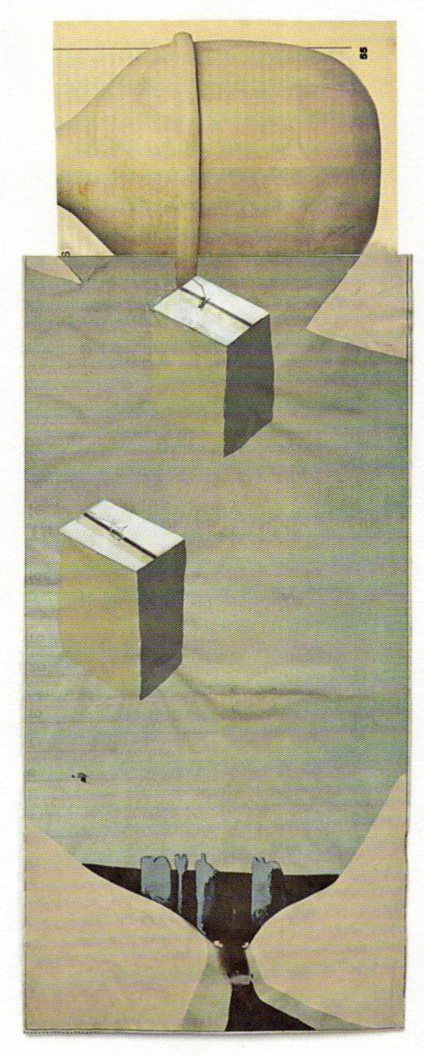

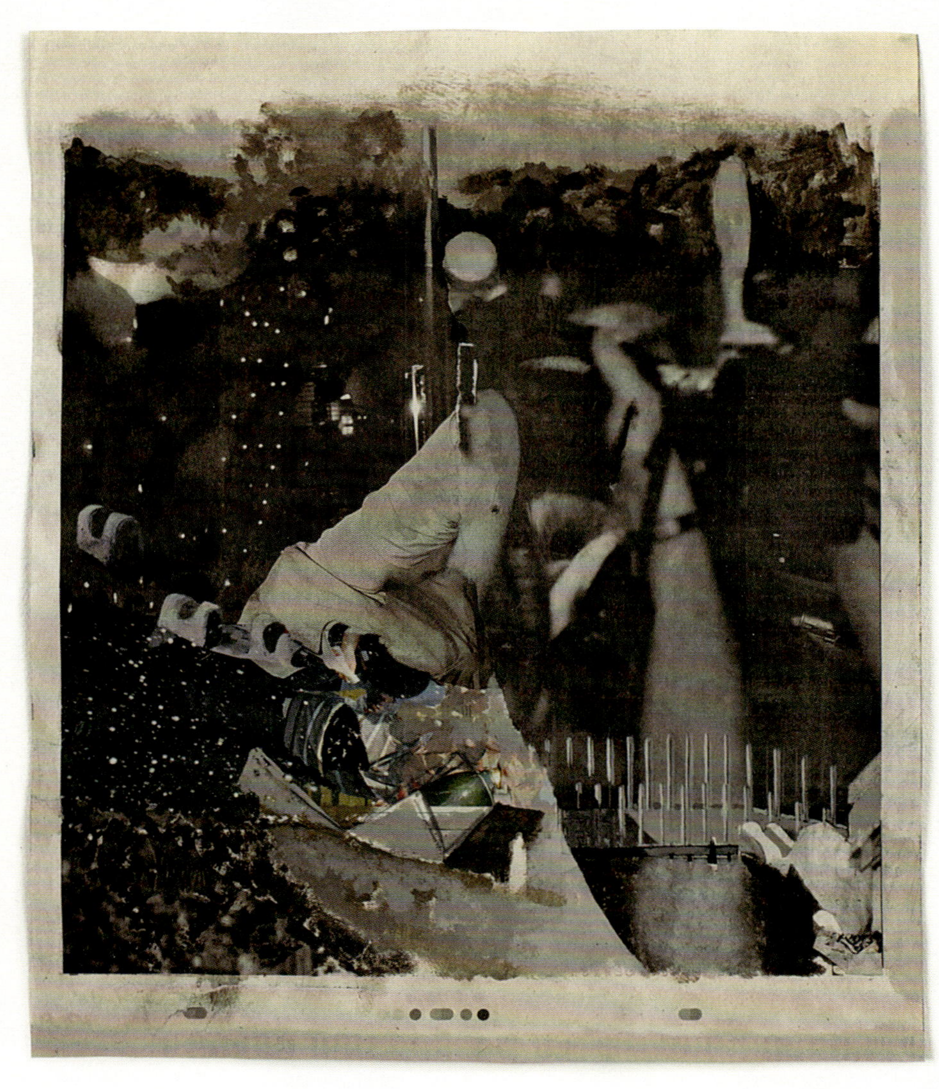

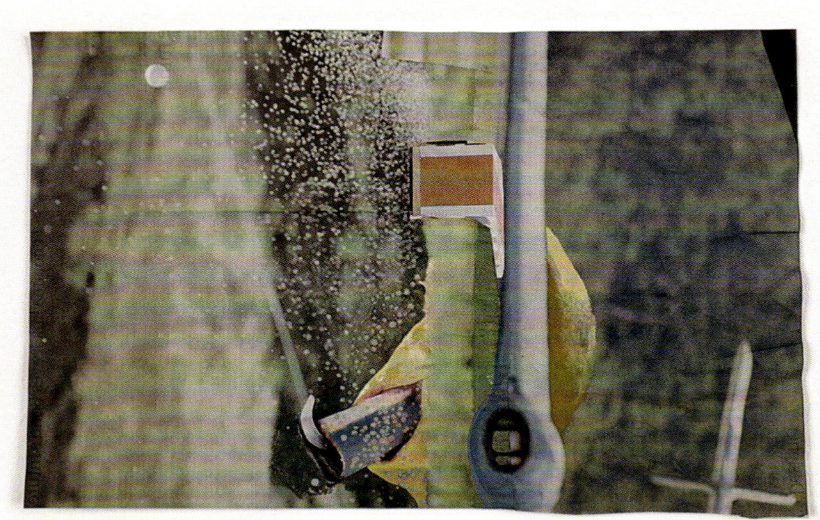

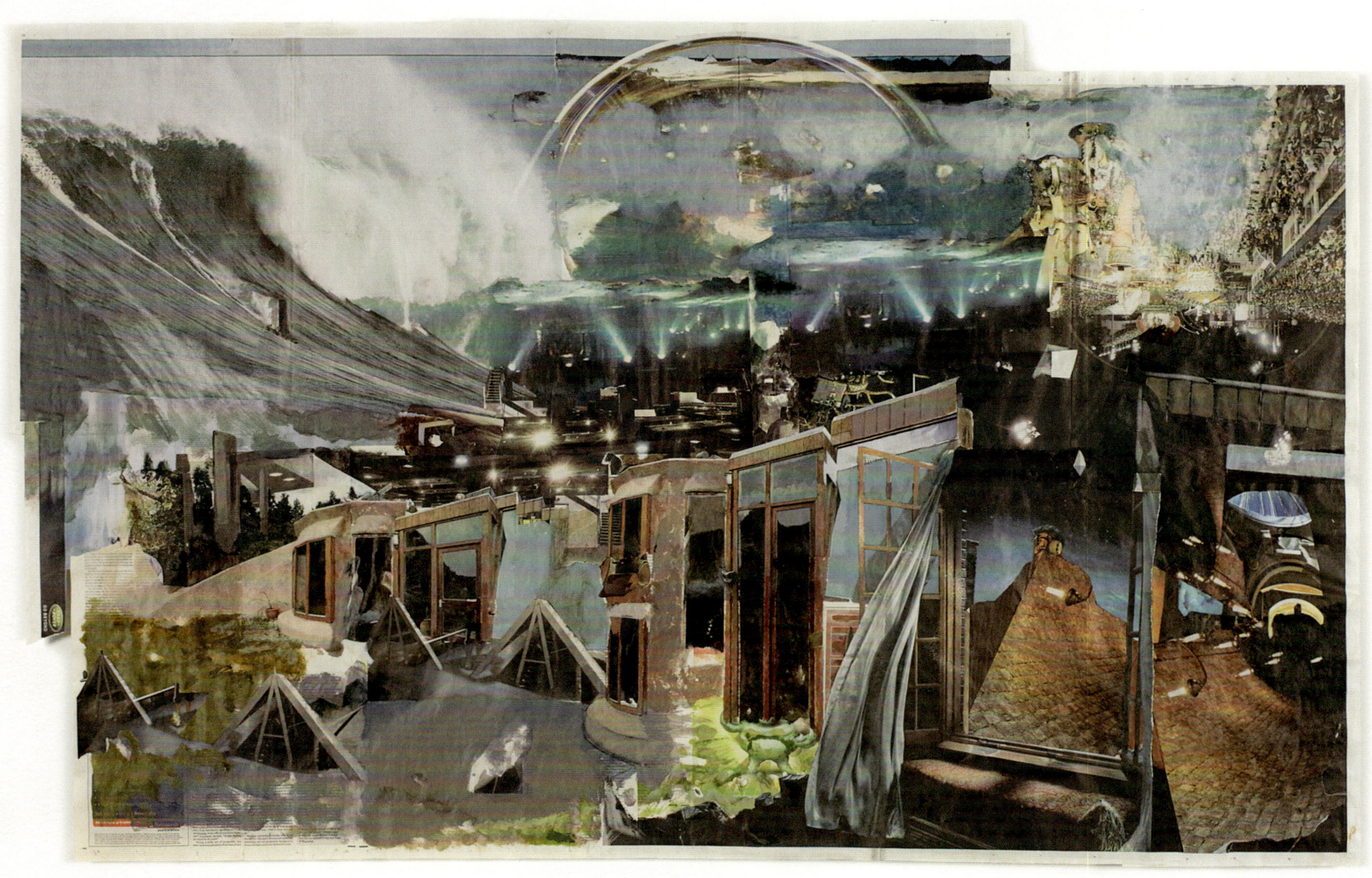

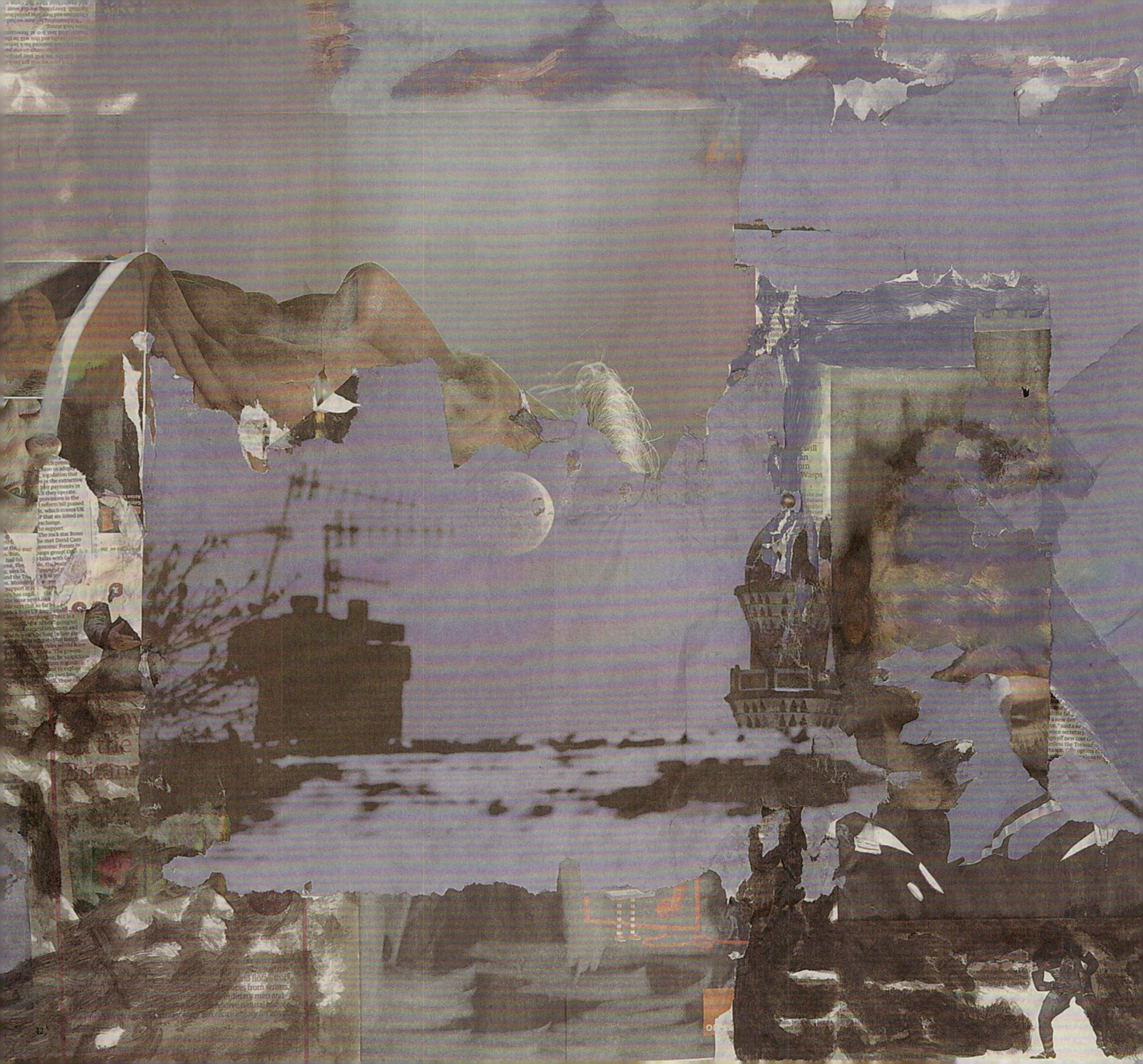

READING THE EVENT: NOTES ON THE WORK OF TONY SWAIN

Isla Leaver-Yap

'A thundercloud passes over; a patch of woodland goes dark – or was it dark already? Who knows? And then, to make it worse, you suddenly come across a block of writing set bang in the middle of the clearing … I can't paint words!' Carlisle's voice raises half an octave.

'Painting's painting, writing writing. Never the twain. It's all wrong, aesthetically speaking: all the depth and the texture of a summer countryside steamrollered into a flat page.'

'That's what I like about it', Serge says.
C: a novel, Tom McCarthy[1]

Tony Swain's paintings primarily 'take place', so to speak, on newspaper. Using this material support as a site in which to reconfigure and overpaint the original content, the artist replaces or blends printed images with painted ones.[2] His paint stitches together fantastical spaces that neither entirely obliterate its original content (the newspaper's familiar registration marks, colour bars and the printed text from the verso of the page are often left partially visible, while the newspaper's photographs become key points for embellishment and painted motifs), nor seek to document a Euclidean reality. Rather, there is a synthesis of document and imagination, external fact and internal thought.

Using the paintings of Tony Swain as its touchstone and inspiration, the following text is a collection of simultaneously recorded observations, short and long, that emerge from reflecting upon the relationship between painting and printing. These two processes, often distinguished by their differences to one other, are instead discussed in terms of how they might abrade together in a productive friction, and how their juxtaposition might generate multiple and perhaps unlikely points of connection. From examining what is at stake both conceptually and practically when paint is applied to a sheet of newsprint, to the linking of artistic practices that illuminate each other by their common interests, these notes are *dérives* that occur in parallel and alongside Swain's work.

The painted page

Key to understanding Tony Swain's work is that it is not painting on canvas, but painting on a page. Unlike the definitive singularity of a canvas, a page is part of a narrative sequence, a member of a quire. Newspaper is a material that asks us not just to look at the image but to read it. Implied, in turn, is the notion that if it can be read then perhaps the image has indeed been written.

Swain's overpaintings begin from an initial detail found within the original newspaper, rather than by a preconceived composition imposed upon the page

which is arbitrary to its original printed content. In this sequential structure, images follow images. The unfolding scene, ribbon-like and serpentine in its process of becoming, is constructed akin to Gertrude Stein's notion of language, where 'one word and another word next to the other word [is] always being chosen'.[3]

That the image might be treated as a text (and, by extension, that painting not always be considered in alterity with printing) should not be surprising. Indeed, the two elements collide throughout the period of Modernism with frequency, from the cubism of Pablo Picasso and George Braque, to the collages of Max Ernst, where such techniques were further constellated and embellished by the coming of Pop Art and the pluralism of postmodernism. And while one can also move in a backward direction and find rich points of image/text interconnection in the role of ornamented text in illuminated manuscripts, let us nonetheless be particular about the material support upon which Tony Swain's images are constructed: newspaper.

Newspaper is the printed page at its most functional: thin enough to hold ink, light enough to carry, cheap enough to mass-produce, broad enough to read. But there is something 'off' about seeing paint on the printed page. The manual application of paint overlaying mechanical patterns admits the jarring relationship between human touch and machine. As if to acknowledge the oddness of its ornamentation, Swain's paint refuses entirely to cohere to the low-grade paper: it puckers and wrinkles; it summons up a strangeness in the image. That the translucency of the paper reveals not only the lightness of the artist's gestural strokes but also the verso of the page is testament to the presence of the 'printedness' of the page – a printedness that, when painted, appears veiled rather than completely concealed from view.

Painted, the page still hangs on to the residues of longing to be read, a habit seemingly hardwired into the materiality of the printed page. But this new reading must take place in a visual vocabulary. In its creative misuse, Swain's painted image wilfully inhabits a form that antagonises its material support, making that antagonism part of its subject matter, its exhibition.

A consideration of rhythm in text and image
By the sixteenth century, the need for mnemonic devices to faithfully preserve elements of collective memory had diminished due to the rise in printing and literacy. Use of cadence, rhythm, repetition and other forms of memory devices were replaced by comprehensive illustration both descriptive and diagrammatic.[4] The printed image began to overtake the oral word. Mnemonic devices slowly lost their use and coherency; they were transformed into dead metaphors, nonsense rhymes and incantatory rituals where function metamorphosed into mythic gesture, artefact. Like abandoned titles, they lacked a context, a clue of their formation. As they became symbol, the uses of rhyme and cadence were transmuted into the medium of imagery, the newly literate visuality.

Ébauche and étude
Traditionally, the process of image-making and the precursor to much painting is the form of the rough outline, the sketch. And within this classic context, the sketch comprised two forms: the *étude*, a study of the subject that acted as an observational record; and the *ébauche*, an initial compositional draft that served to translate the artist's initial idea

for a composition into a more elaborated version. Put simply, where the *étude* serves as a mere document of reality, moving outwards from the artist, the *ébauche* is a record of the imagination that synthesises what one has received within the mind.[5]

Responding to Paul Nash's painting *Event on the Downs* (1934), art critic E.H. Ramsden noted, 'It is not the painting of a landscape that concerns the artist, but the transcription of a mood'.[6] Here, Ramsden's emphasis is less on Nash's attempt to create a painted copy of the physical landscape, and more on the way in which he appears to translate the idea of what takes place within that site into image as one might try to record a dream. This is the imaginative transcription of an event unfolding, it is the painting of an image reflected in the mind's eye.

While Nash's *Event on the Downs* prioritises the formalisation of the *ébauche* as a finished artwork, the paintings of Tony Swain describe a fluid movement between the two types of sketch. Swain's work takes the material subject as the primary apparatus through which to present the field of painting (where both the newspaper's materiality and its printed content are prerequisite triggers for the development of a painted image in the abstract). His paintings seek to draw the real and surreal into dialogue with one another; both states are made present, contingent on each other for meaning.

The consequence of such a dialogue is that the generated images are a lyrical reimagining of the printed page as a subject in possession of an unconscious desire, a page that dreams of itself beyond the confines of its literal definition. An imaginary document, the artwork is revealed to be in possession of an auratic potential, an abstraction that is an exhibition of desire.

Swain collapses the ephemeral, fleeting newspaper image with the flash of the internal mind. The process of painting extends the duration of that flash. Taking the initial printed detail as a starting point for the development of a painting, the artist's images find the breaches, the jumping-off points from the reality

of the printed page. His images tug and unpick the newspaper's imagery, expanding its hallucinatory qualities as it dreams of itself as image.

Three other artists
The accidental printer. Despite his frequent use of newspaper print in his work of the 1930s and 1940s, Willem de Kooning claimed he cared little for it on a conceptual level. As if to deny the qualities of the material, the artist described his painting on newsprint as accidental, the product of a merely functional endeavour. He would often use paper to mop up excess paint and hasten the drying of the canvas. When removed, the newspaper would leave its imprint on the image. And yet de Kooning played down the significance of this image transferral. This personalised, albeit haphazard, printing press was denied by its printer.

The flatbed painter. It would take de Kooning's ardent follower Robert Rauschenberg to admit newspaper's significance as a legitimate material for painters in the early 1950s. Fascinated with the newspaper techniques of de Kooning, Rauschenberg would use newspaper to prime his canvases, so that the printed material might activate the ground of his paintings.[7] Experiments in dissolving the printing ink into his paintings allowed Rauschenberg to recast the newspaper as a collective *wunderblock*, embedded and reified within the classical medium of paint. His startling combinations of paint and print declared the performativity of the newspaper.[8] Critic Leo Steinberg often compared Rauschenberg's canvases to a flatbed printing plane, the horizontal bed that supports a printing surface. The flatbed allowed for a plurality of positions and perspectives by flattening each element into a single plane,[9] images made contingent by proximity rather than intelligibility. The process allowed painting to enter into the realm of collage previously inhabited only by printed matter and photography.

The zero painter. Following Rauschenberg's newsprint image transfers, the veracity of the newspaper image as material was again contested and extemporised by Sigmar Polke in the 1960s. Similar to the work of his contemporary, Roy Lichtenstein, albeit with a drier humour, the German painter enlarged, distorted and reconstructed raster patterns newspaper's then-form of image printing which comprised clusters of Benday dots that gathered to form photographic impressions. In contrast to the seriality of Warhol's silkscreened canvases of Hollywood starlets and gruesome reportings of roadside accidents, Polke painstakingly hand-painted each Benday dot and consequently rerouted the casual repeatability of the mechanical press into the durational process of the painter's touch. In a typically dry acknowledgement, Polke knew the primary symbolic element of the raster doubled as both circle and zero.

Images dictated by print

At the dawn of the printing revolution, the rigidity of typographical possibilities within the standard printing press directly affected the production of imagery; the machine dictated the means by which images might be created, reappropriated and comprehended.[10] Printed images, for example, did not proliferate with the same speed and variety as the printed word. In the Nuremberg Chronicle (1493), a woodblock print of Mantua was reused to represent Verona. And later, in that same chronicle, we see an illustration serving as a portrait for two different men, Baldus and Lorenzo Valla. Visual cliché expanded as a consequence of a dearth of new imagery, and placed urgency on the need for new visual vocabularies.

Given the rigidity of the image, and the rise of cliché, there is a sense in which the image is a highly resistant element. It possesses wholeness. Irreducible to the same extent as moveable type, the image refuses to be derailed quite as easily as text and, even in its reappropriation, an image can't seem to let go of as much context as a word or even a phrase. It exhibits its origins yet.

Print and the event

'Press': it is not by accident that we use the same word for both the people and the mechanism involved in newspaper publication. With 'press' there is no differentiation between the authors and the machine. In each case, the word describes the effect of the contact that occurs between contingent elements – a collision between the things that generate the newspaper, a fugitive pattern of information made material, developed under great pressure.

As if by alchemy, the press' application of ink transforms blank pages into the depiction of an event. This is content as event – the pronouncements of things made newsworthy for the reason that they lack the character of the pedestrian, the everyday, the banal. The press constructs the newspaper as an everyday product that nonetheless denies 'everydayness' by only choosing to print the remarkable event. As Maurice Blanchot notes with a certain horror, 'In the everyday, everything is everyday; in the newspaper, everything is strange, sublime, abominable.'[11]

The press does not merely find events that take place, but in its dissemination, the press *takes up* time and generates history. In its process of printing, newspapers not only make events for public dissemination, but they also put events in the 'just-past'. This just-past is the not-quite-history, an event whose recorded unfolding is still tangible through its ripples. In its daily reportage, the press dictates the length of an event to those who do not participate in its coming.

Painting, meanwhile, is a preservation. The presence of a painted image serves to encourage contemplation without the urgency of the fugitive event. Indeed, painting requires us to return to its presence over time. It has the capacity to conceive of new lines of time,[12] in order that its meaning might resonate through history and acquire different meanings, experiences.

Swain's paintings repurpose the 'eventfulness' of the press. Speaking only in terms of its formal qualities, his paintings are full of flat light. Without any adherence to single point perspective (that might mobilise the logical patterning of shadow), his paintings produce a vacuum of time; these collaged viewpoints do not produce an image with multiple temporalities, but rather generate an image of time without end. The architecture of the painted space occurs outside of time, providing a different route to the strange, sublime, abominable – an event in an unreasonable space.

Notes

1. Tom McCarthy, *C: a novel*, New York: Knopf, 2010, p.146.

2. When printed text is occasionally visible in Swain's paintings, it appears more as a means of introducing tone than for the display of a word or a linguistic pun.

3. Gertrude Stein, *Look at me now and here I am: writings and lectures, 1911–1945*, Patricia Meyerowitz (ed.), London: Peter Owen, 2004, p.42.

4. Elizabeth L. Eisenstein, *The Printing Revolution in Early Modern Europe*, Cambridge: Cambridge University Press, 2009, p.98.

5. Peter Galassi, *Before Photography: Painting and the Invention of Photography*, New York: Museum of Modern Art, 1981, p.20.

6. E.H. Ramsden, 'Paul Nash: Surrealism in Landscape', *Country Life*, 2 January 1942, p.28.

7. See Grégory Picard's 'Advancing the Artist's Legacy', an interview with Ealan Wingate, *Artinfo.com*, October 2011; and Leo Steinberg, 'The Flatbed Picture Plane', in *Other Criteria: Confrontations with Twentieth-Century Art*, Oxford: Oxford University Press, 1975, p.85.

8. Carolyn Lanchner, *Robert Rauschenberg*, New York: Museum of Modern Art, 2009, p.7.

9. Steinberg, op.cit., p.82.

10. Elizabeth L Eisenstein, *The Printing Press as an Agent Of Change*, Cambridge: Cambridge University Press, 1980, p.255.

11. Maurice Blanchot, *The Infinite Conversation*, trans. Susan Hanson, Minnesota: University of Minnesota Press, 1993, p.243.

12. See Claire Colebrook, *Gilles Deleuze*, London: Routledge, 2001, p.62.

Isla Leaver-Yap writes and organises projects about contemporary art. She is based in New York.

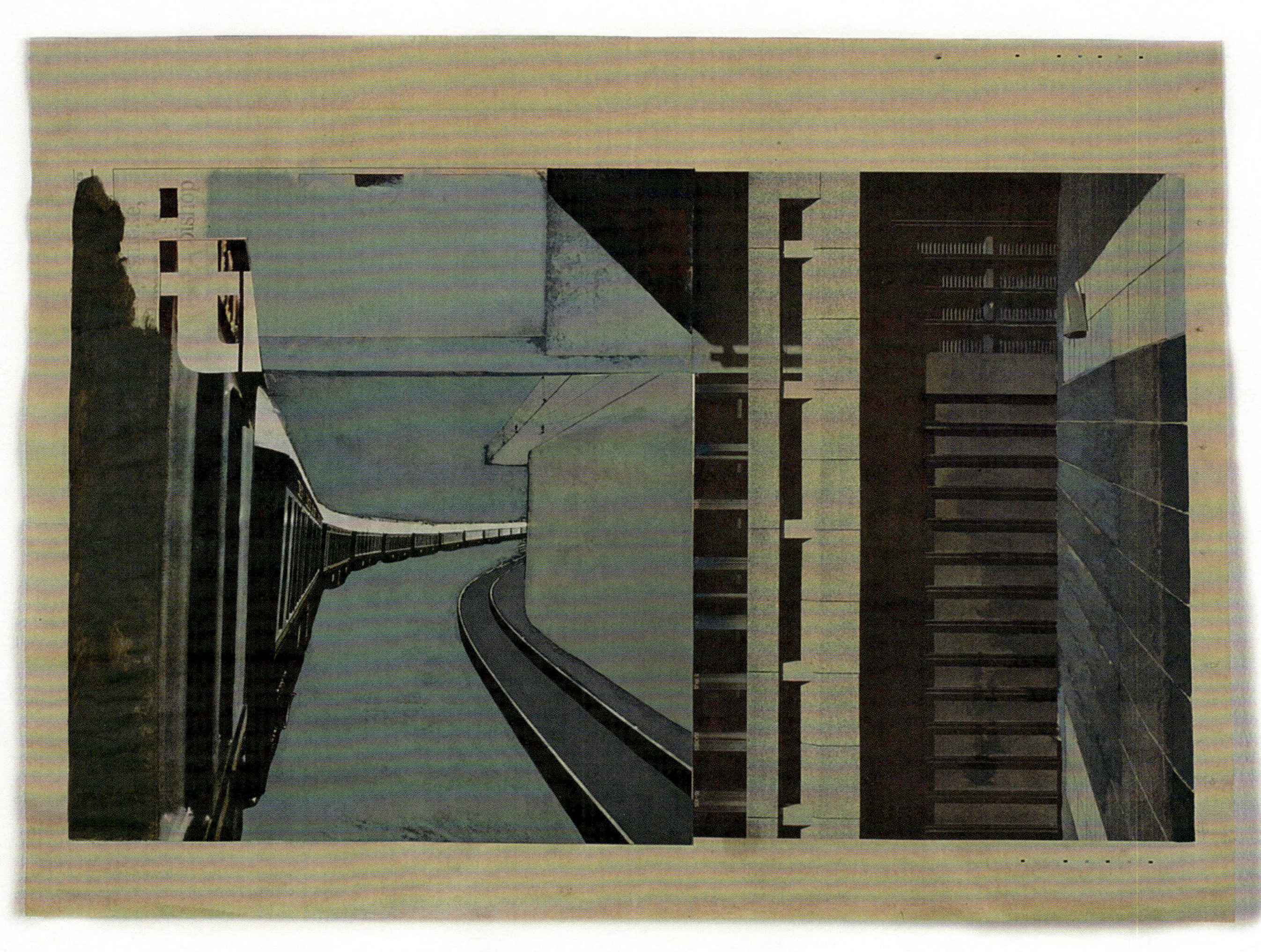

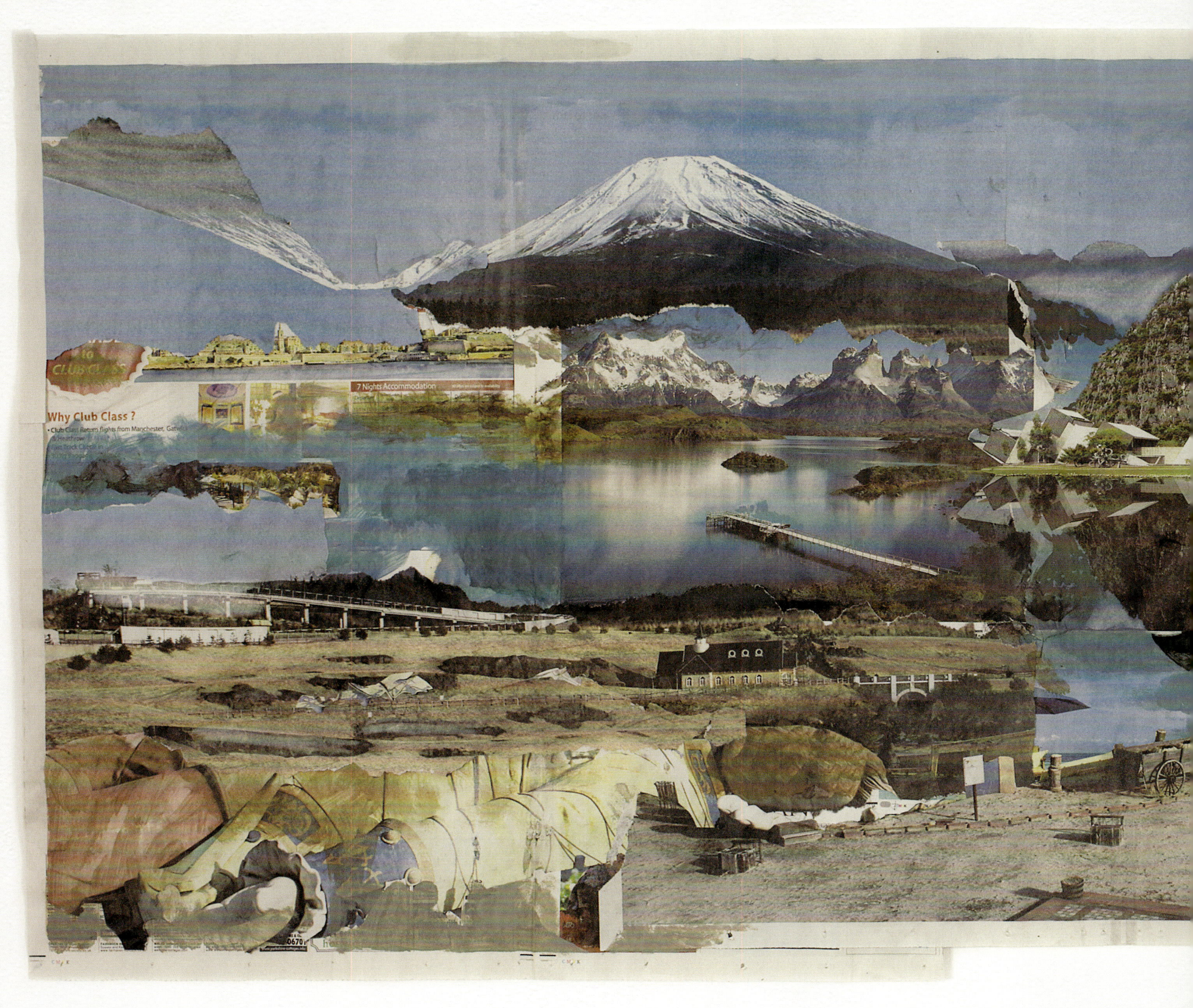
to
CLUB CLASS
7 Nights Accommodation
Why Club Class ?
• Club Class Return flights from Manchester, Gatwick
& Heathrow

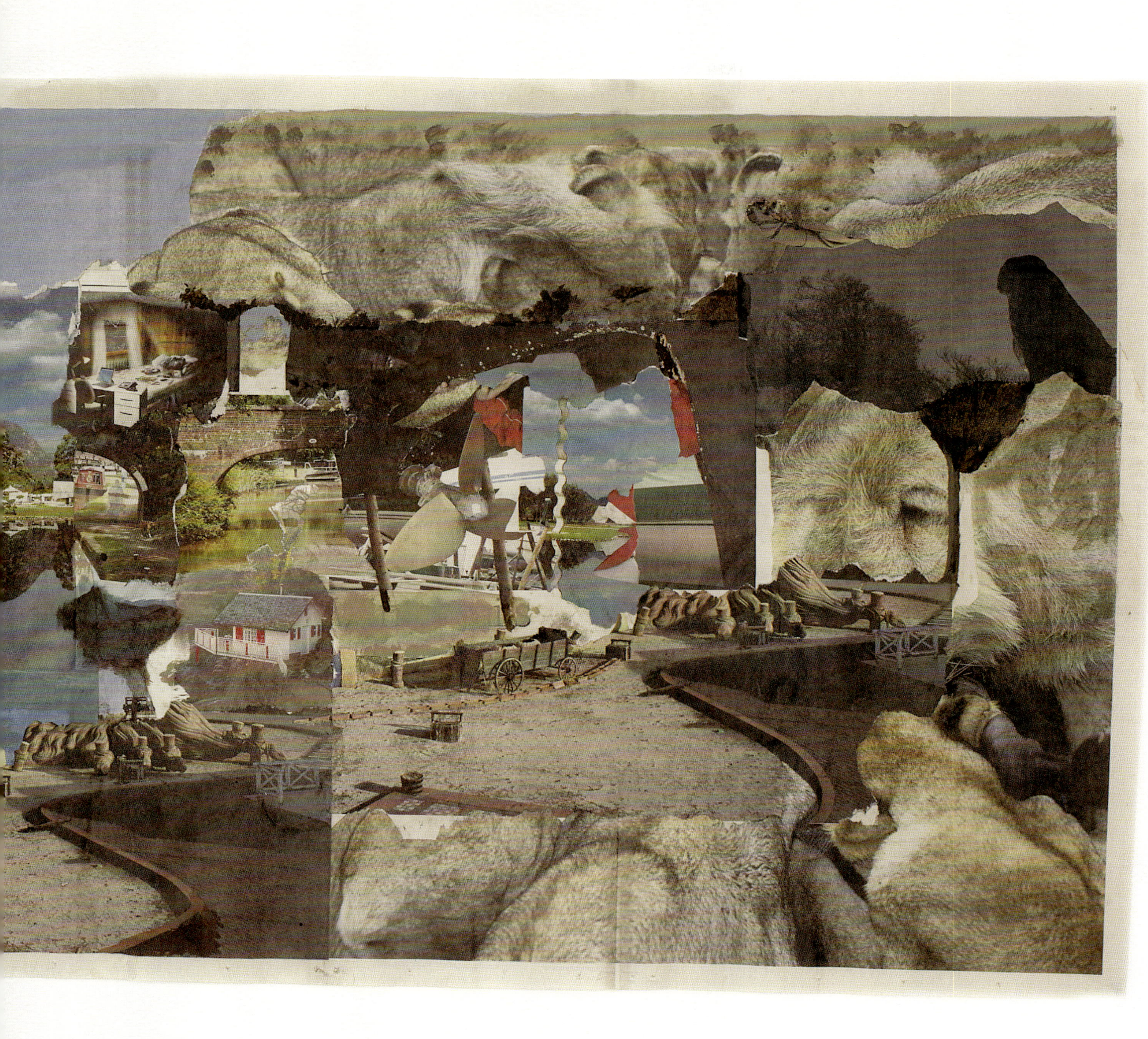

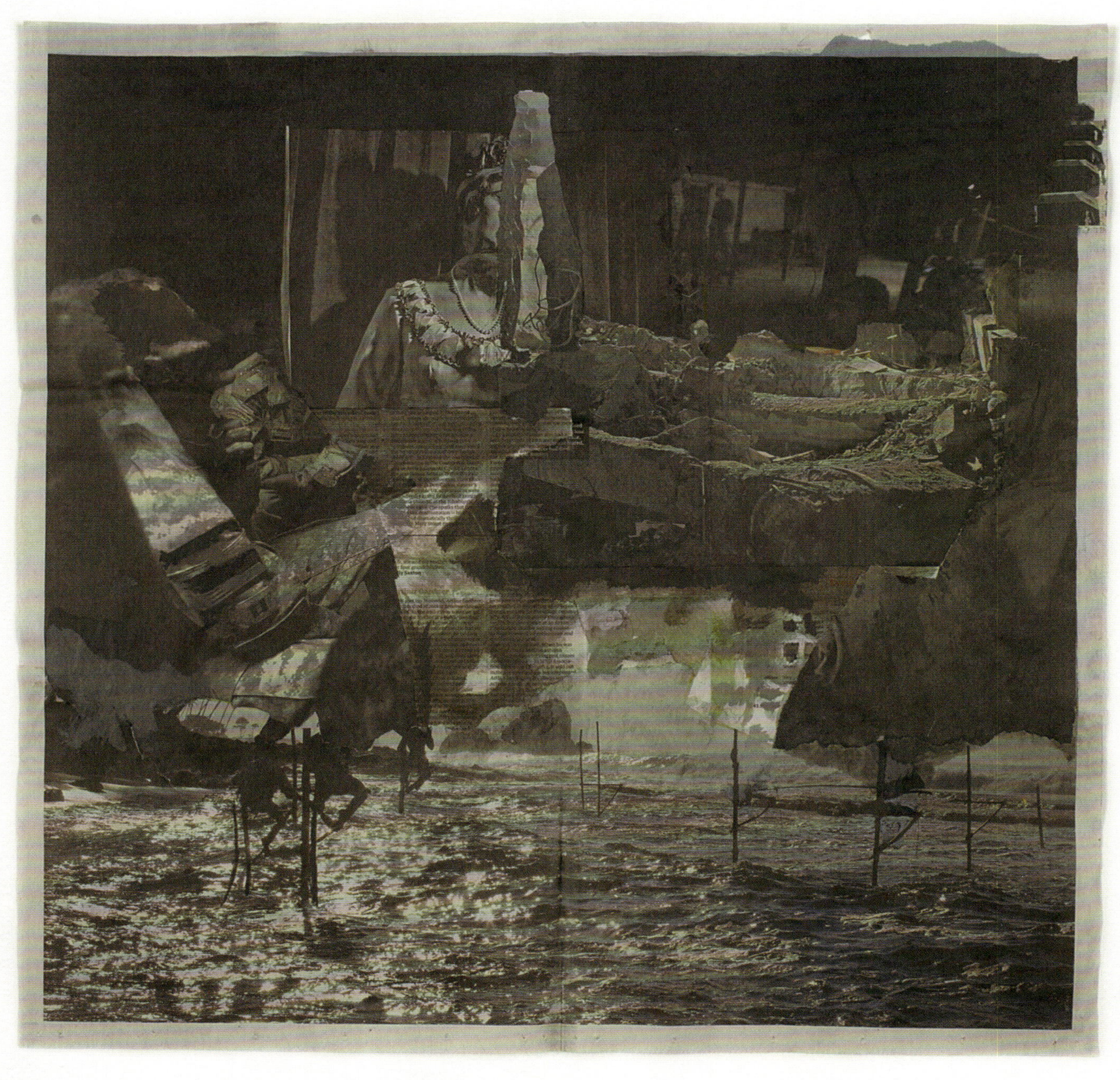

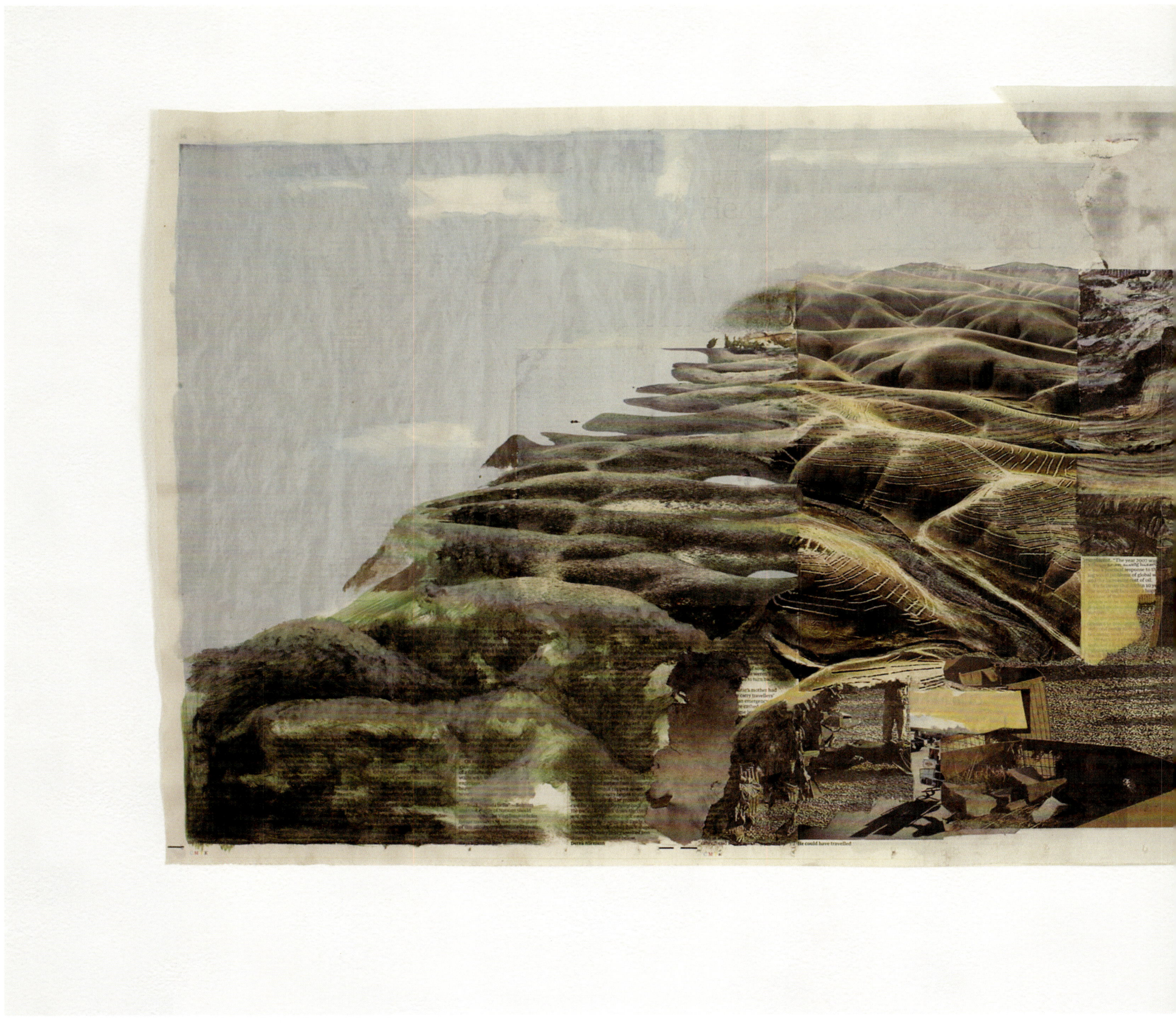

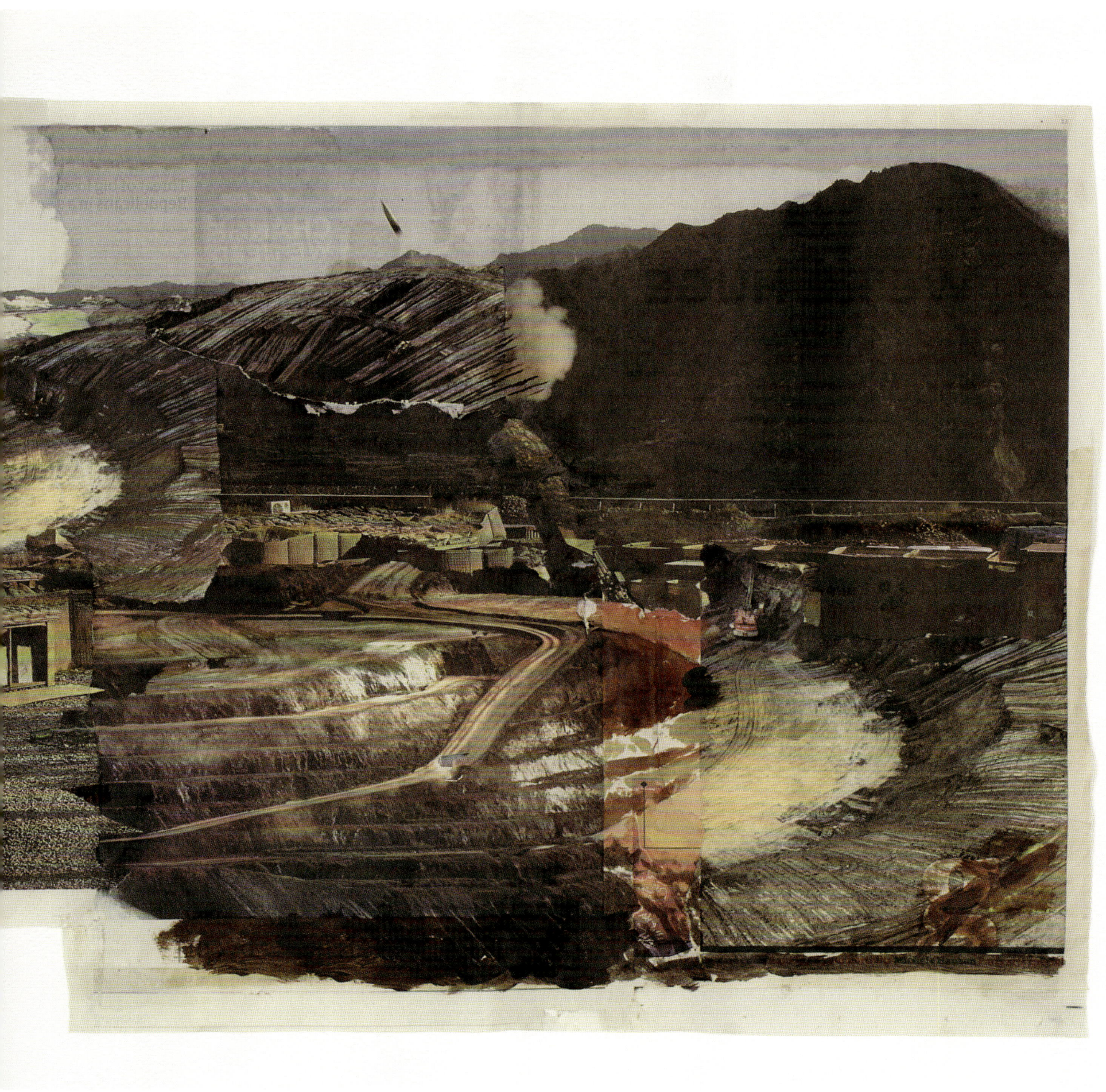

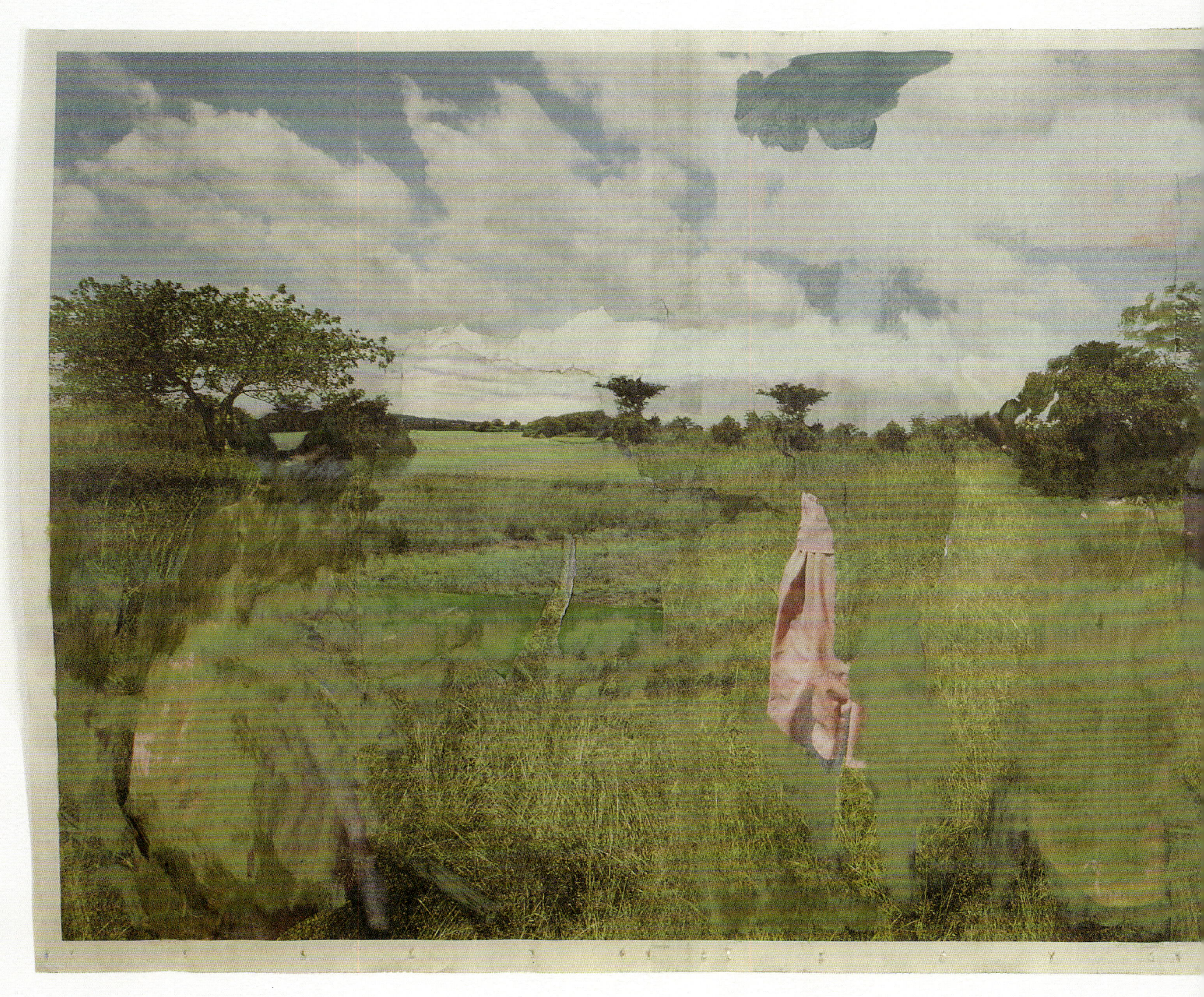

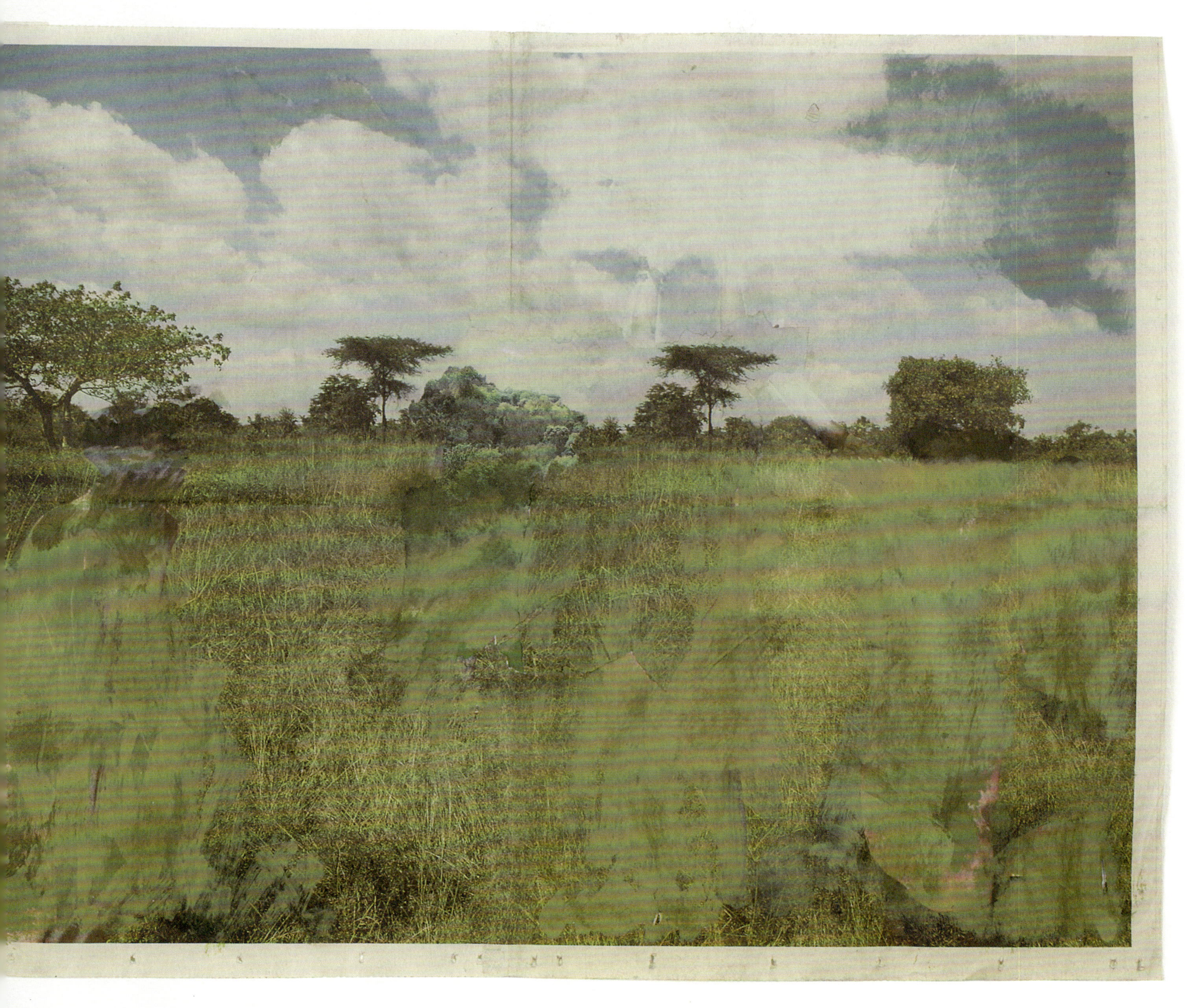

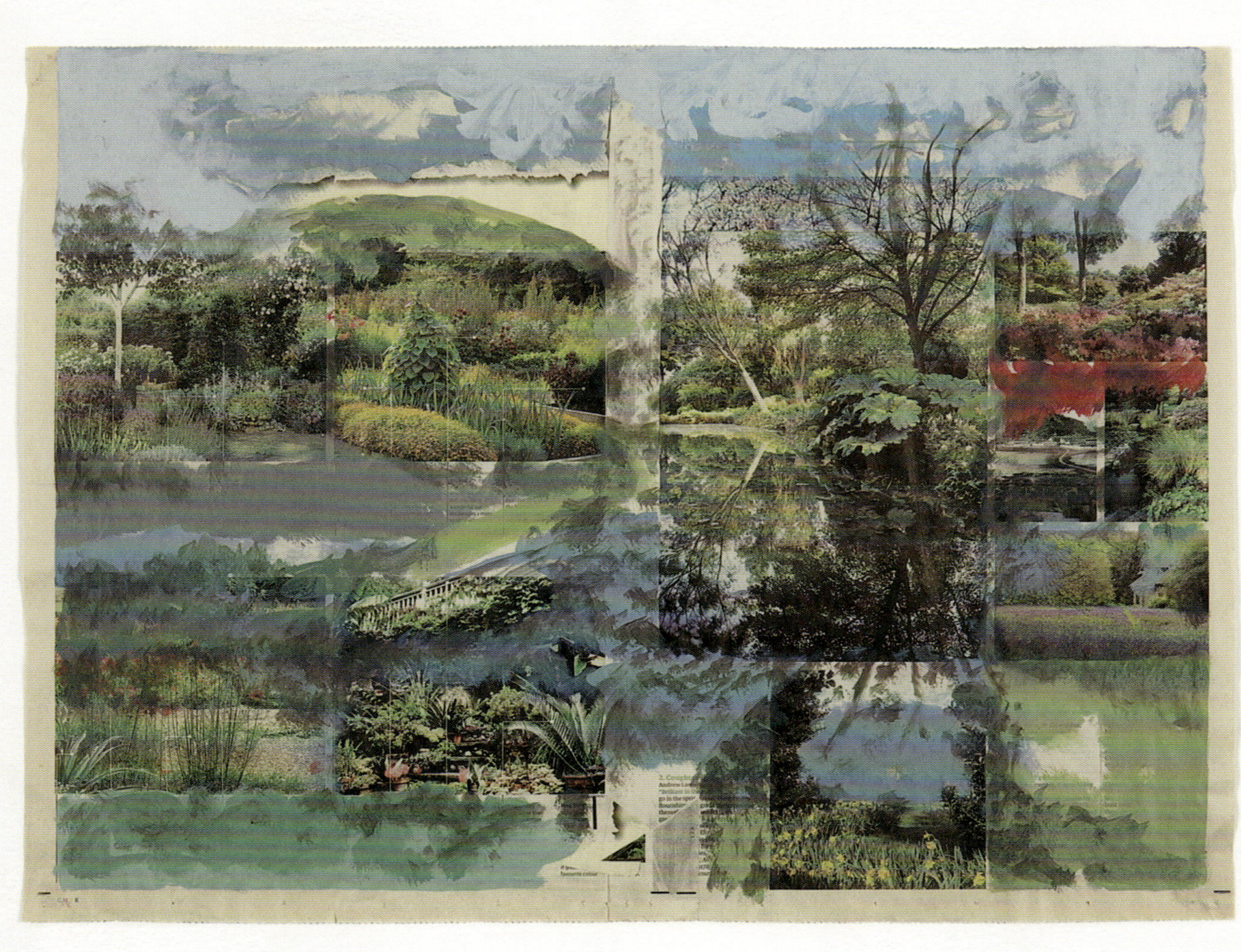

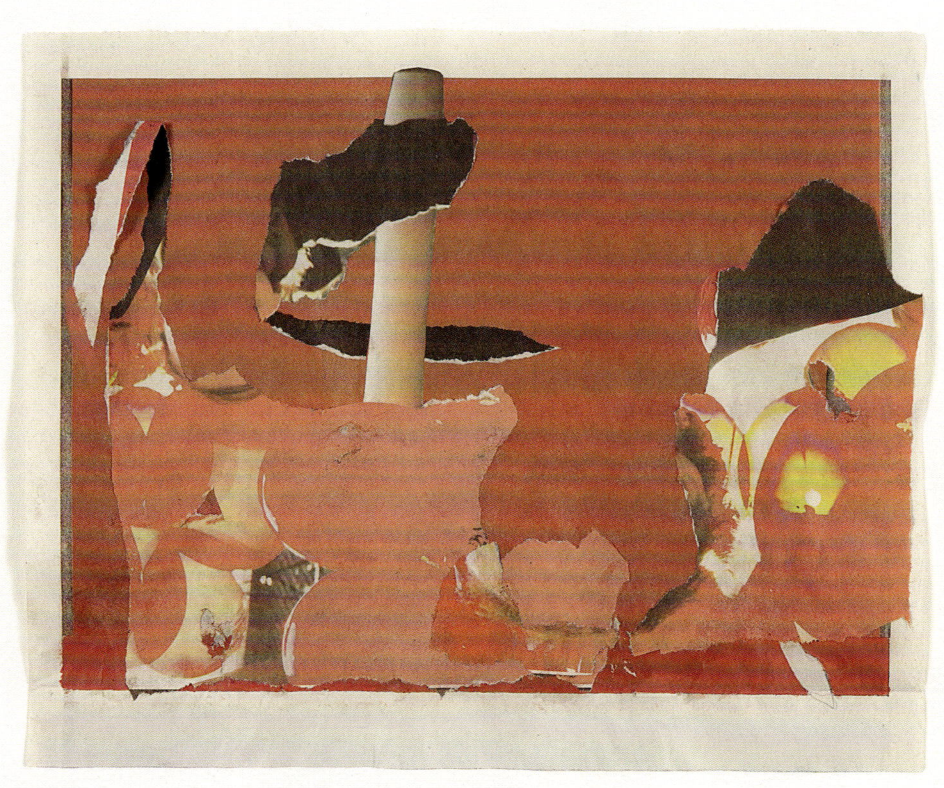

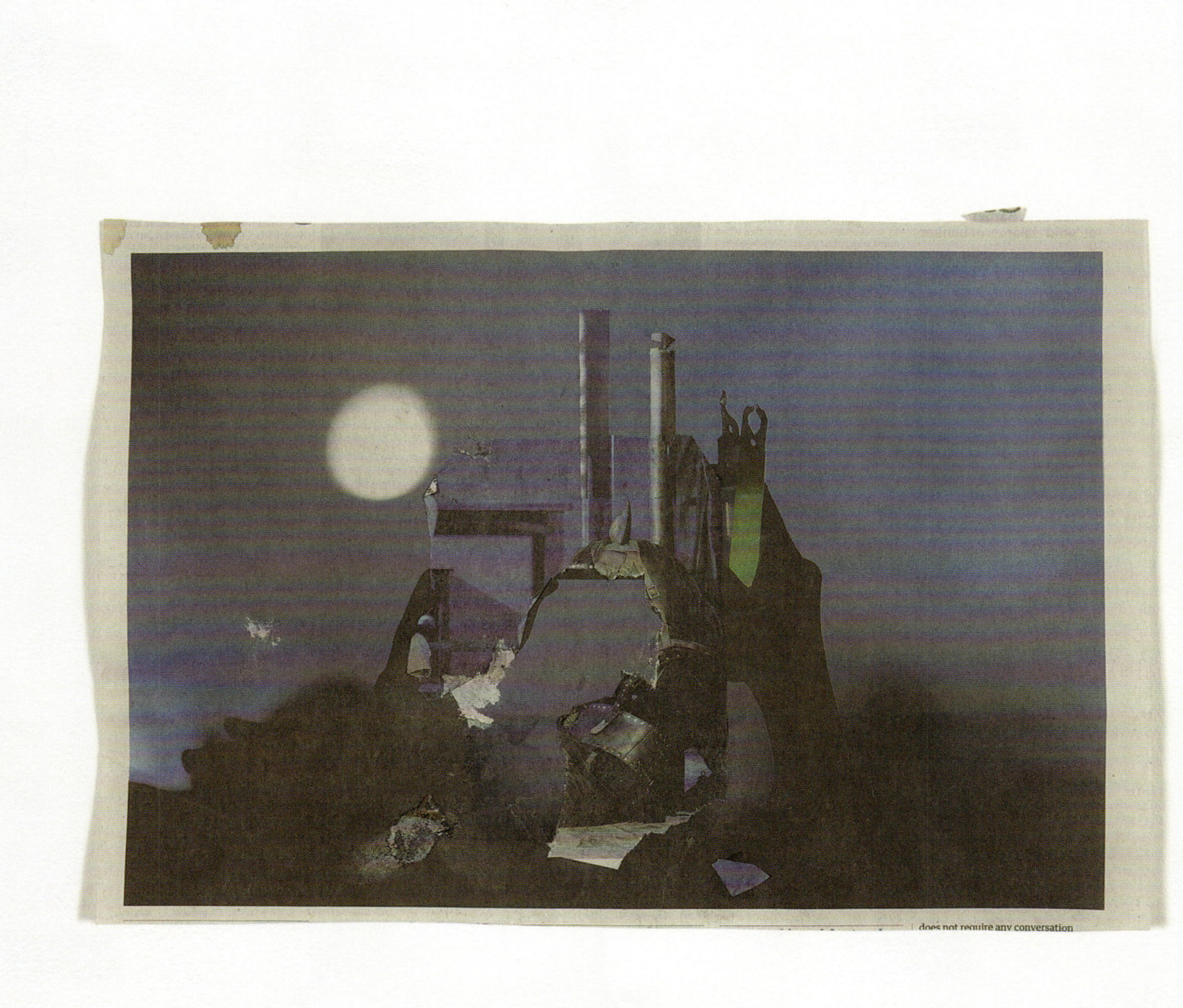

does not require any conversation

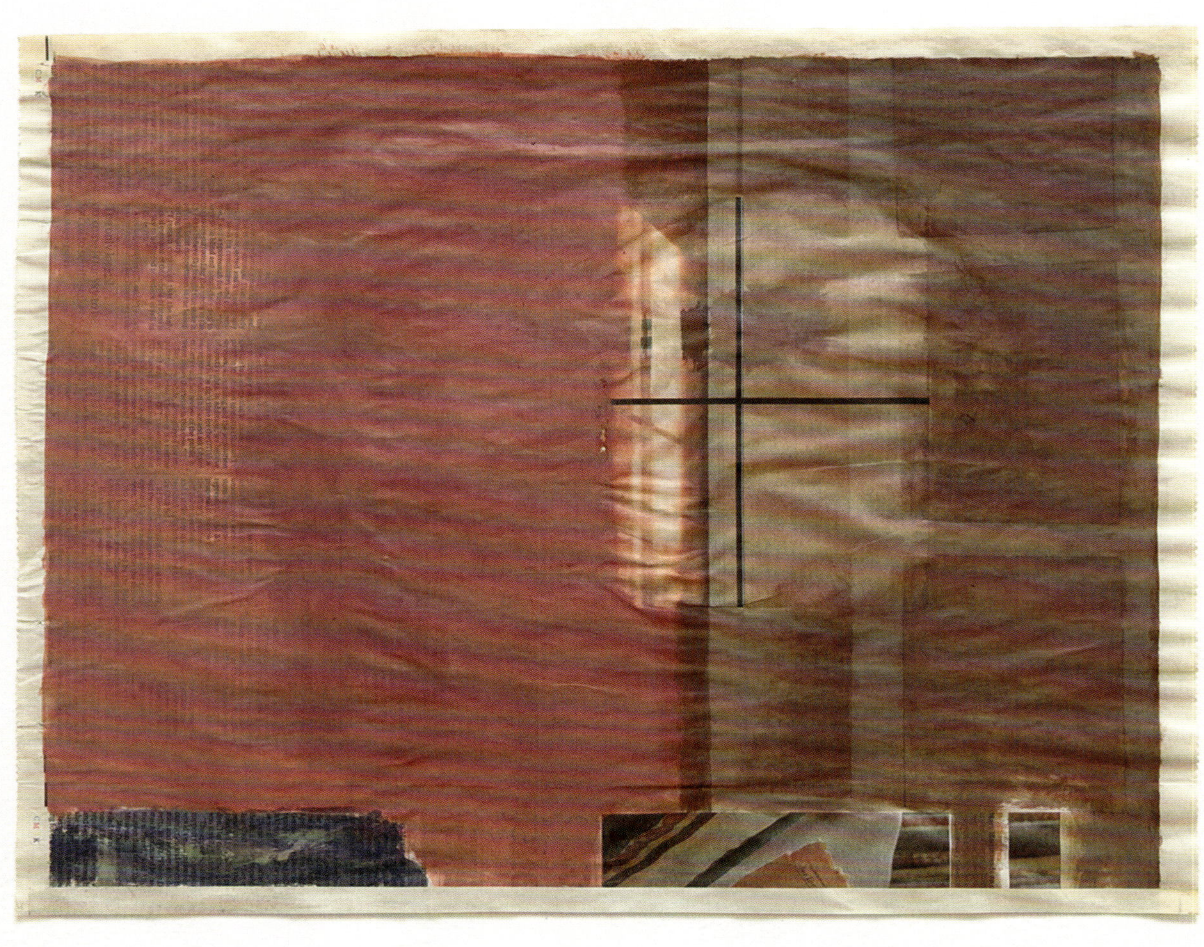

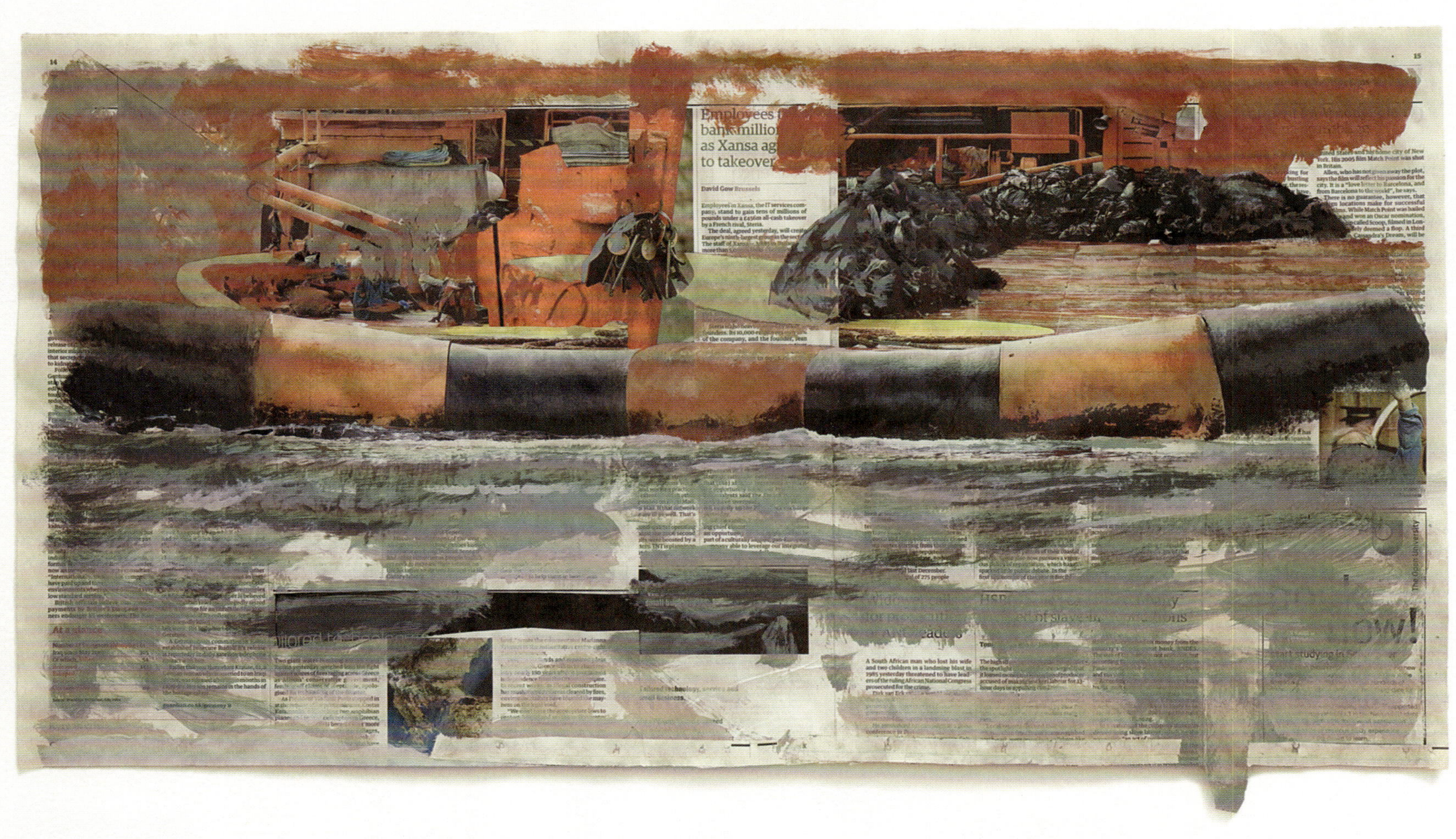

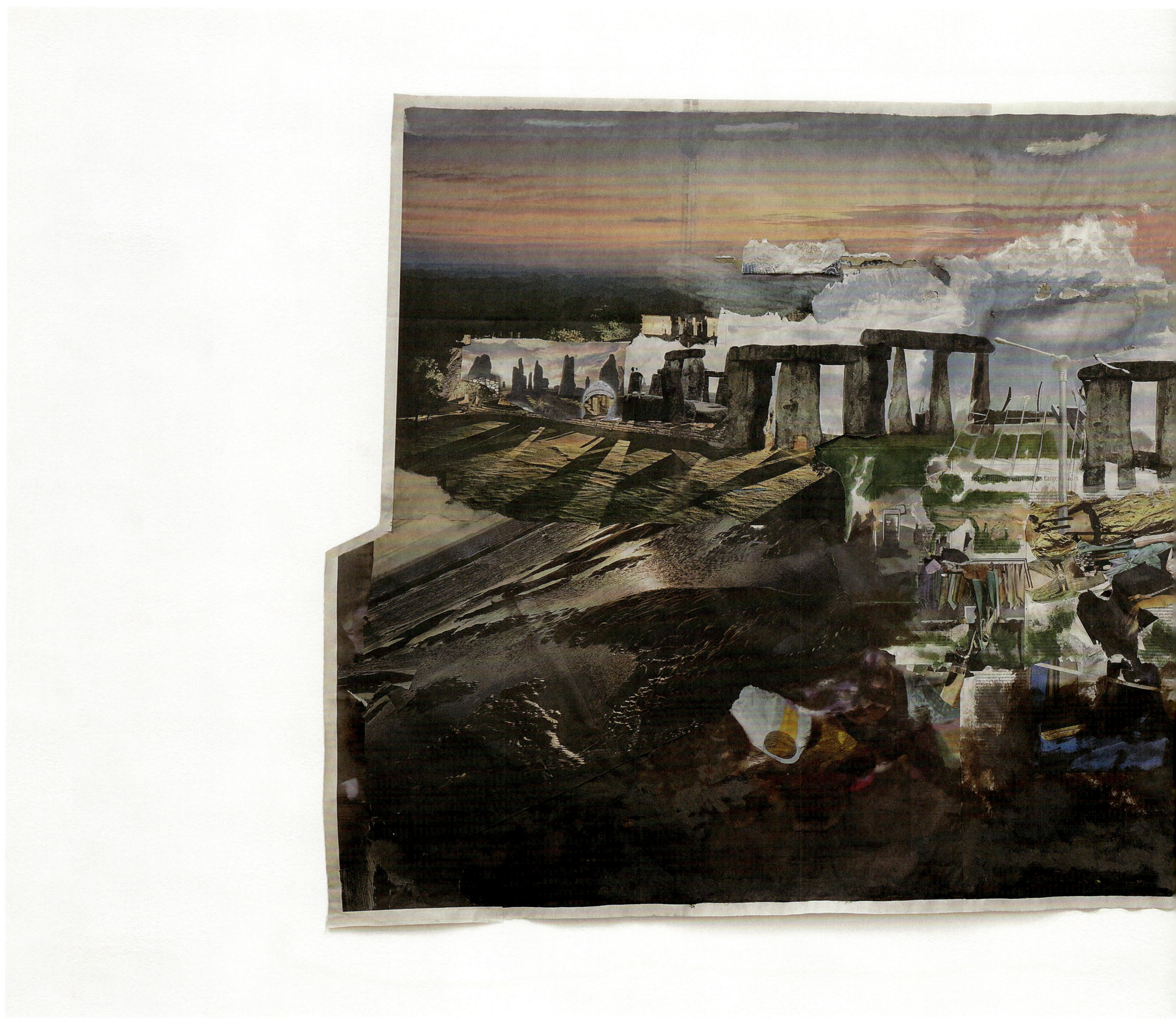

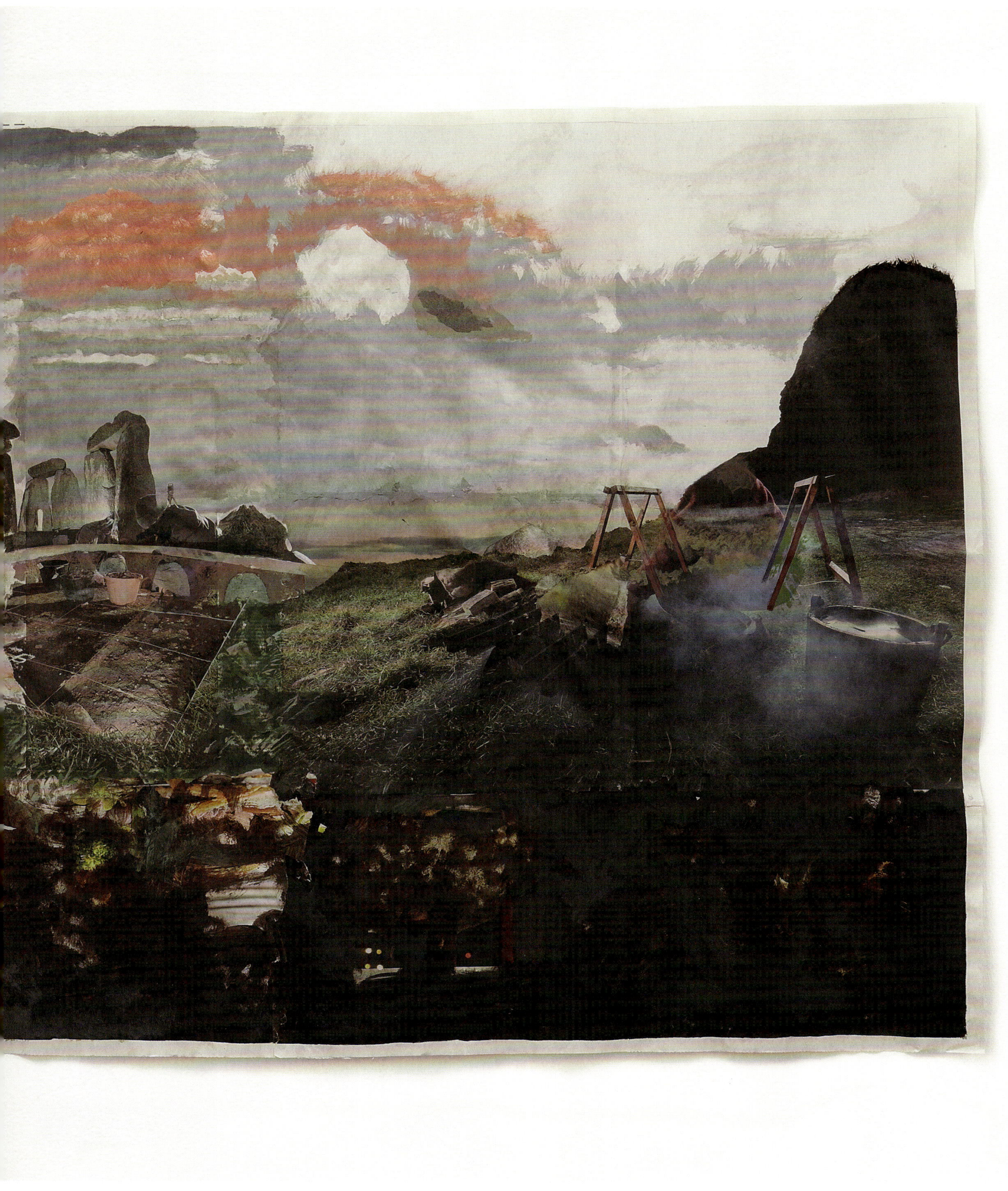

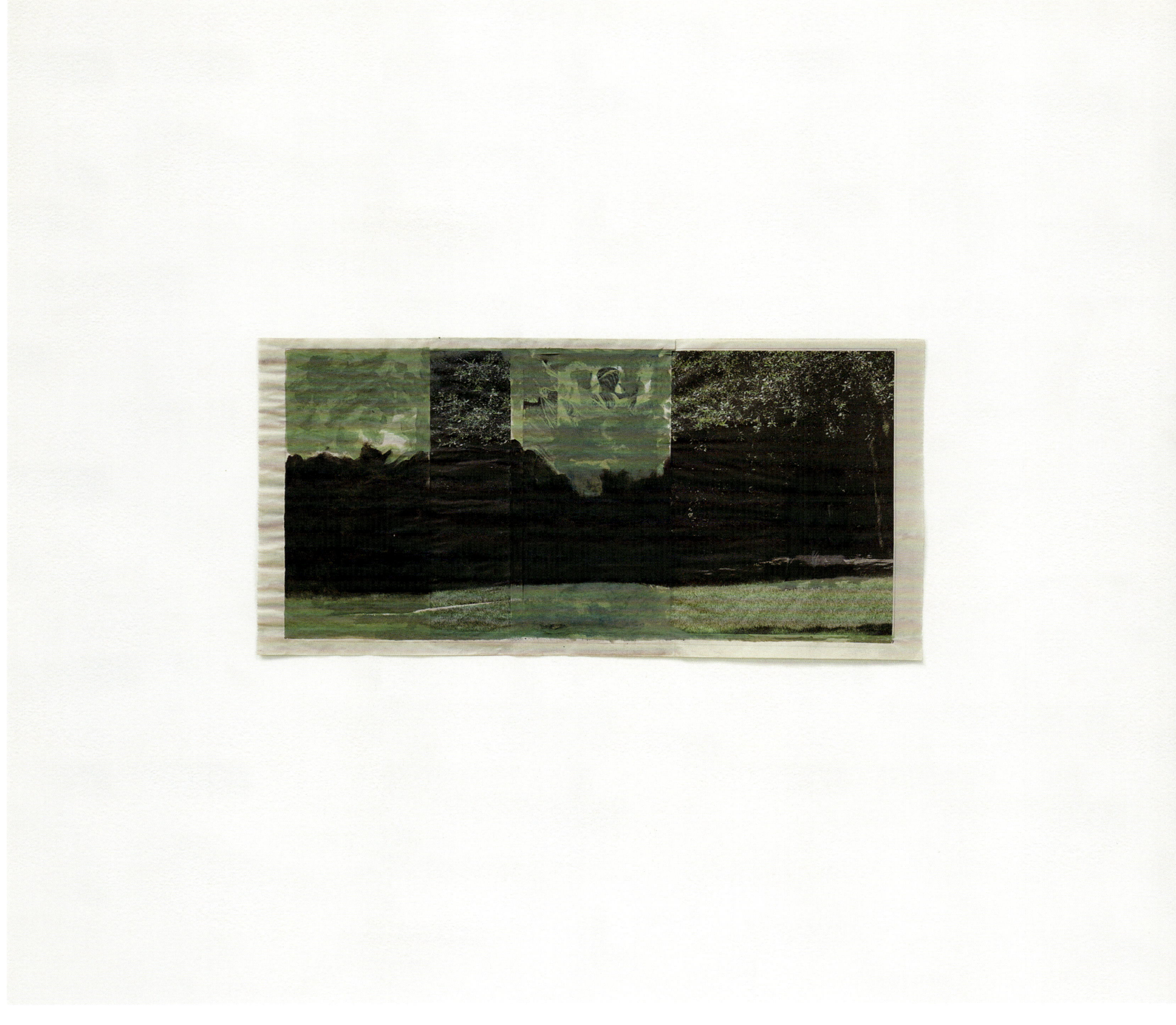

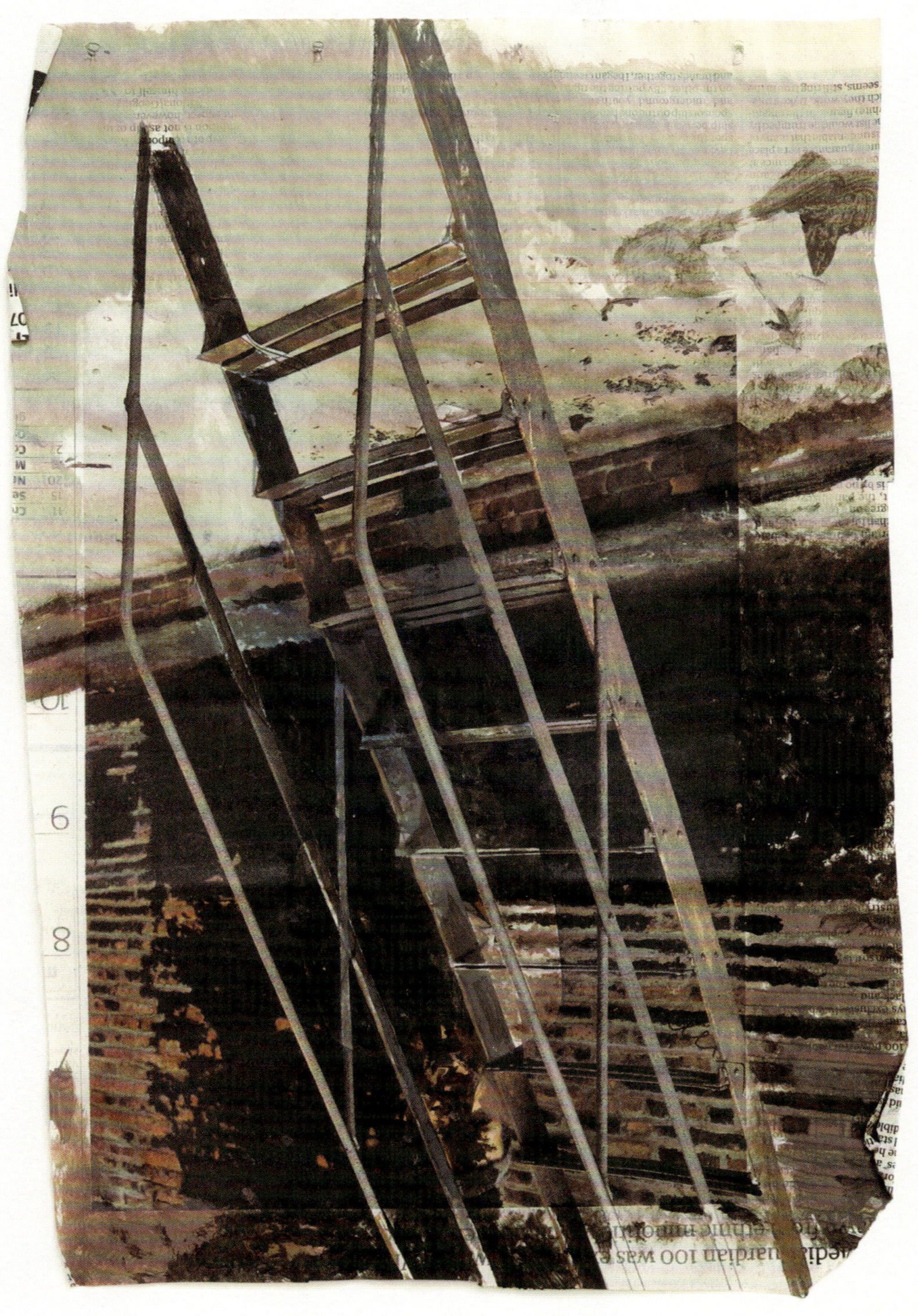

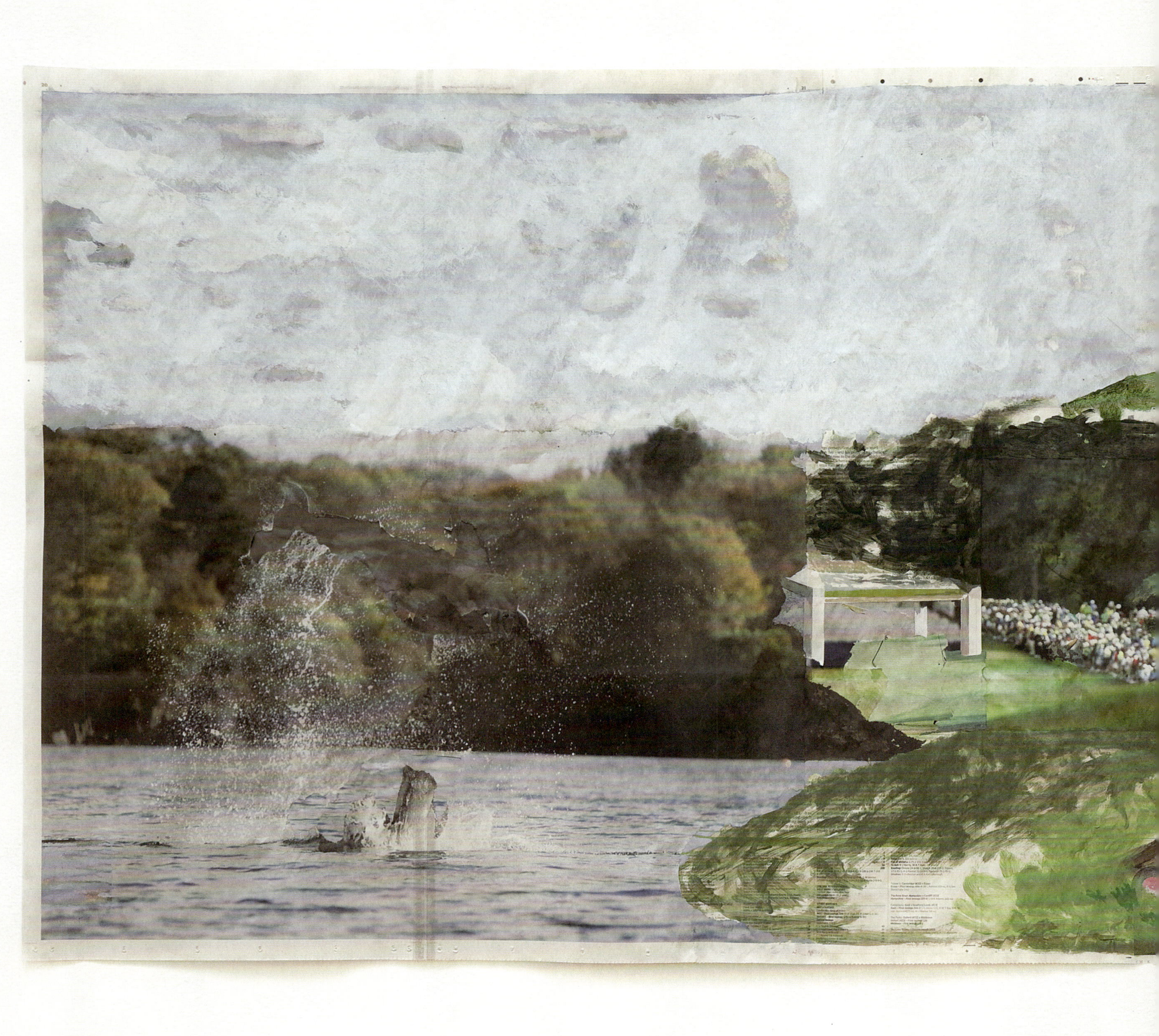

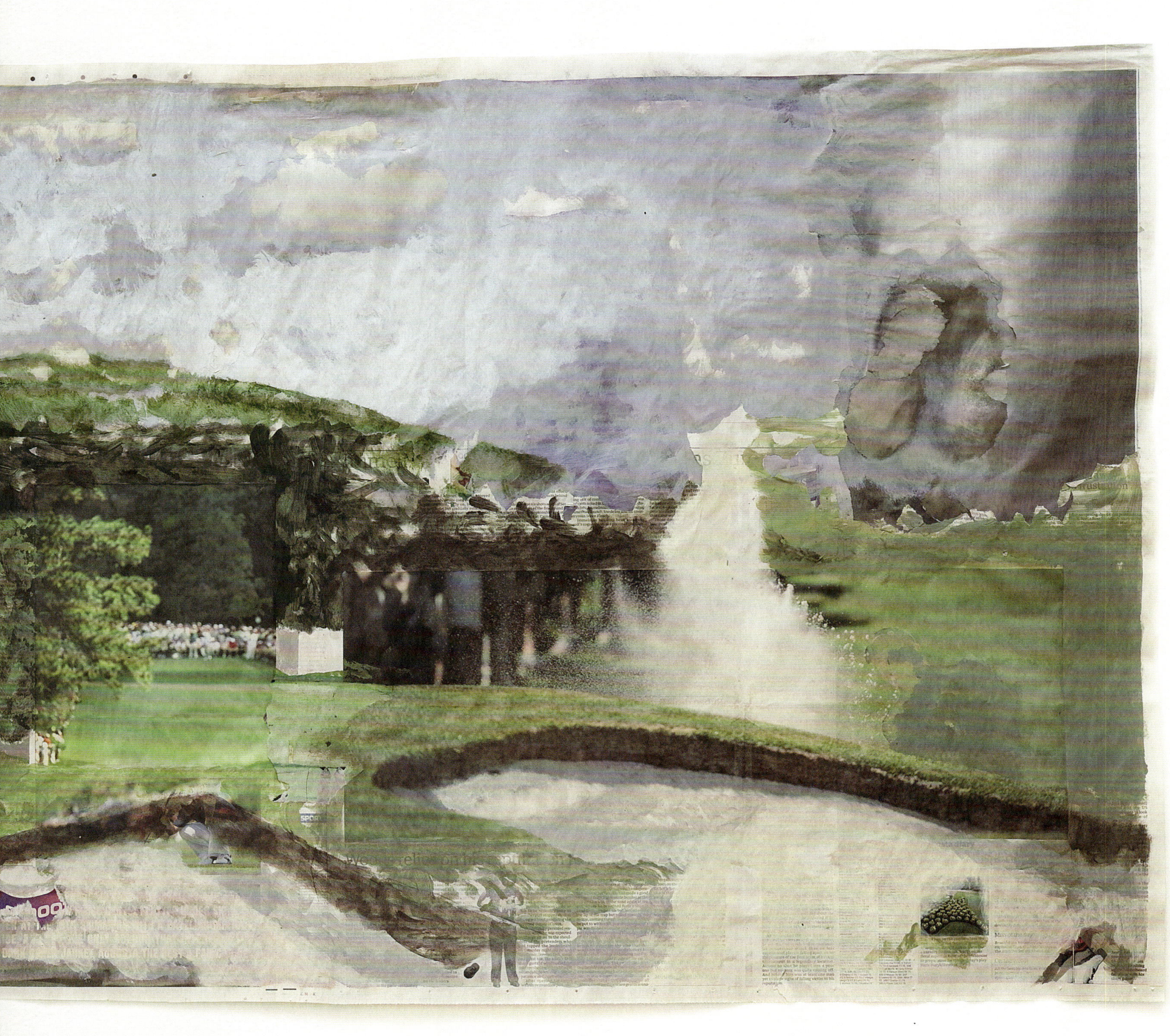

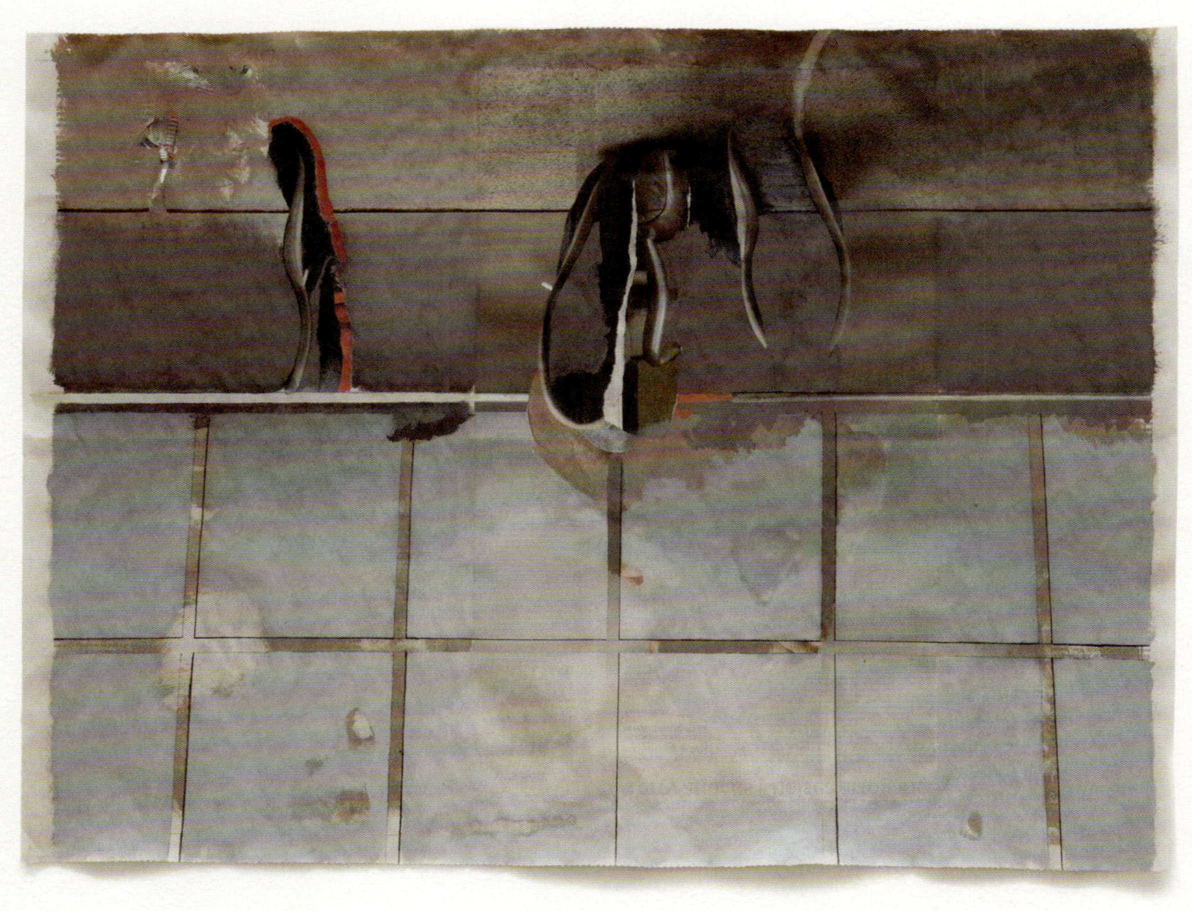

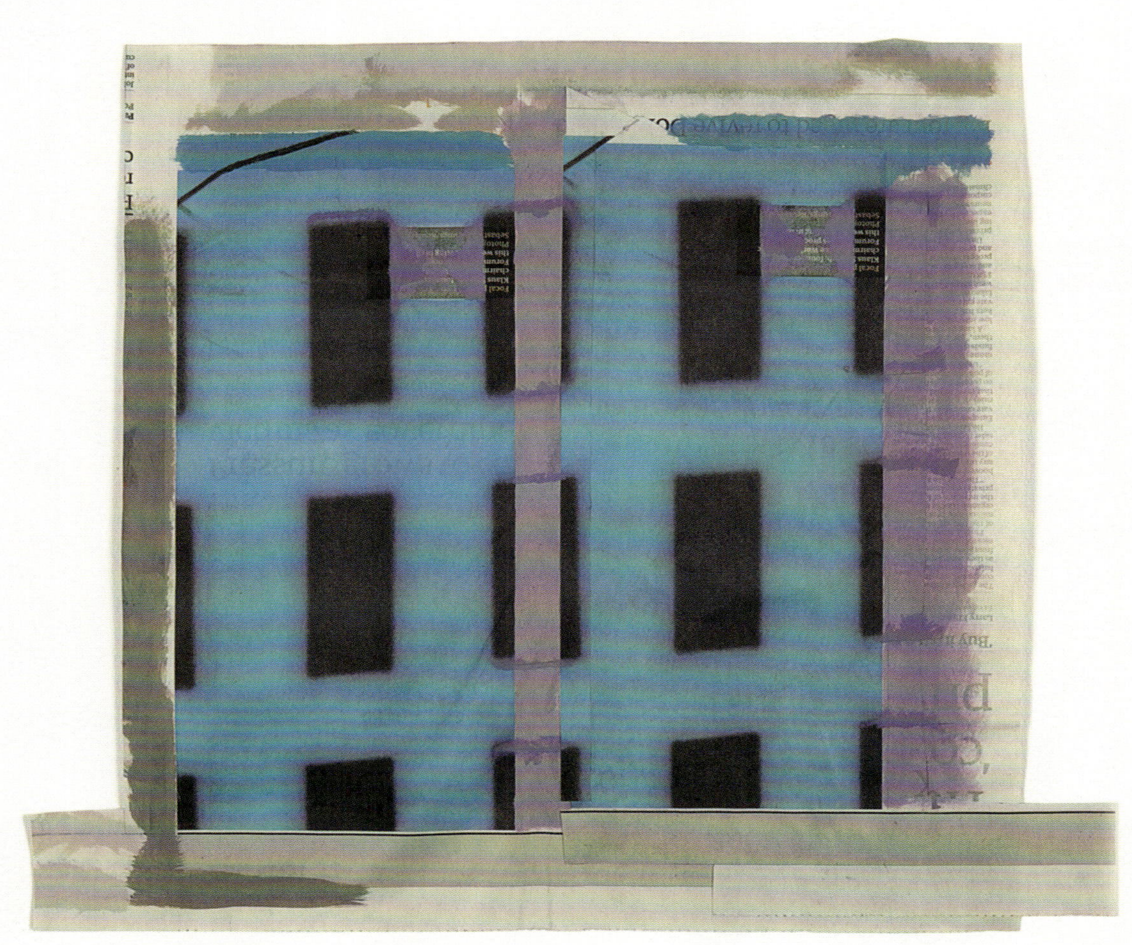

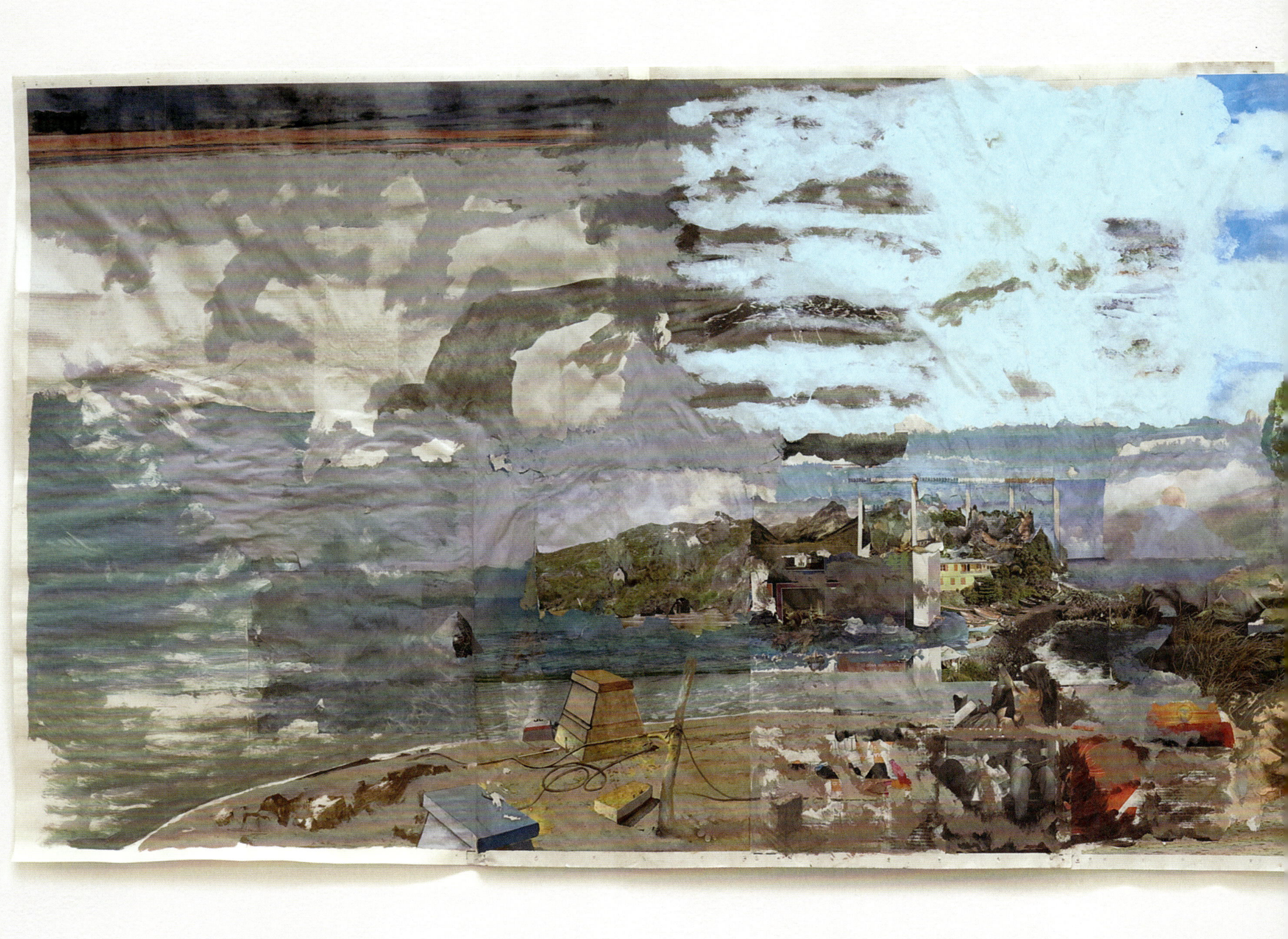

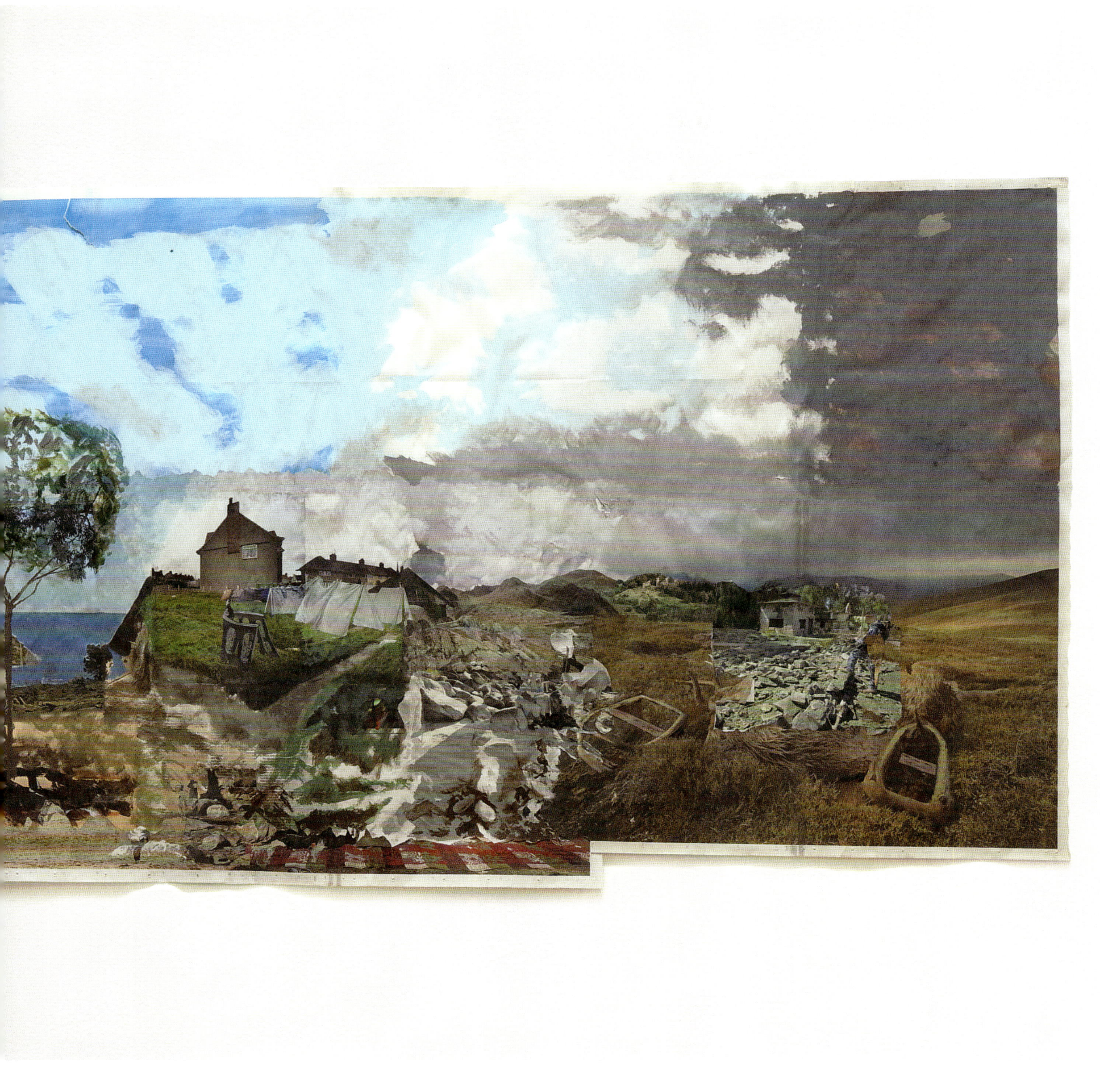

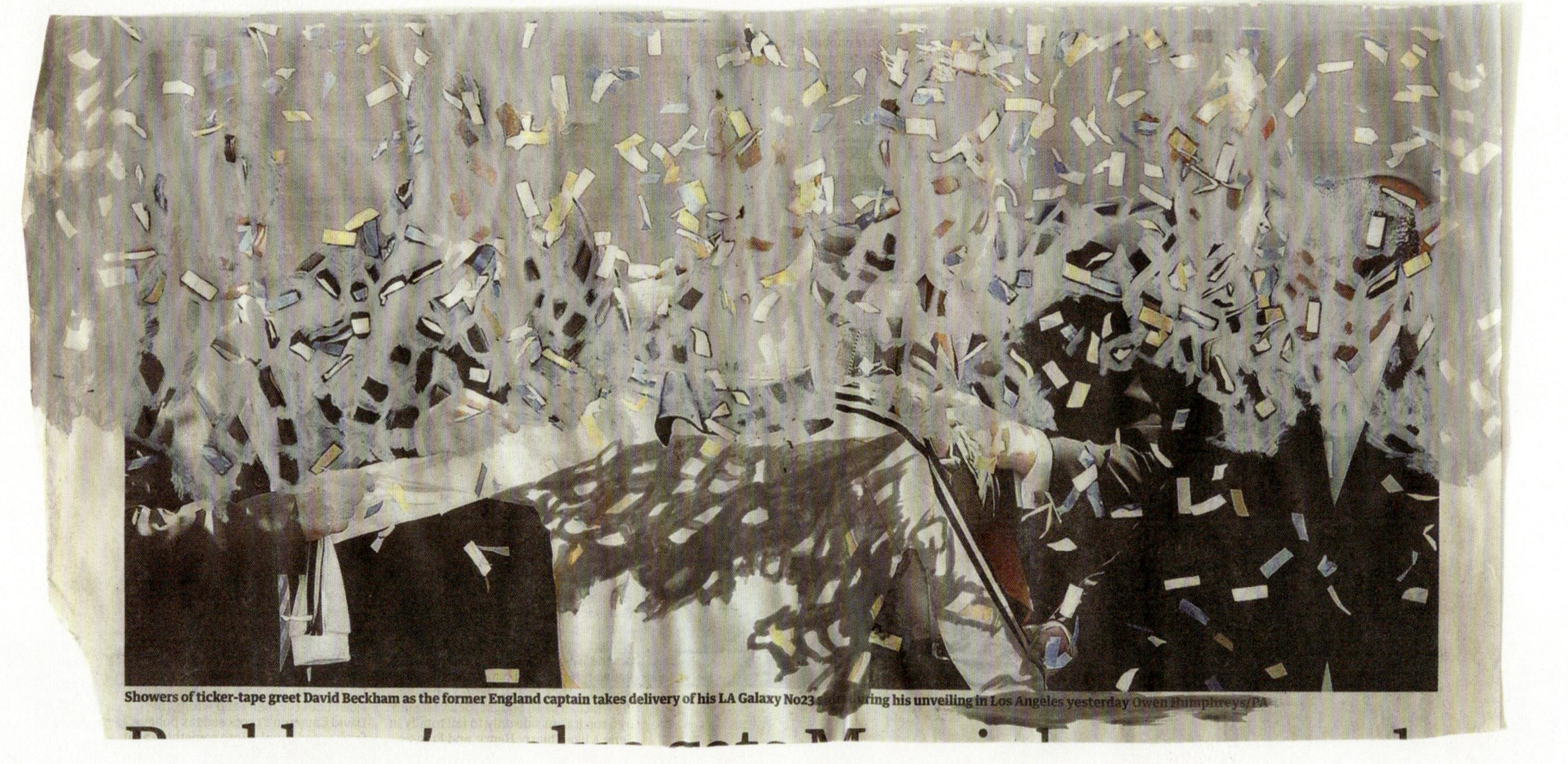

Showers of ticker-tape greet David Beckham as the former England captain takes delivery of his LA Galaxy No23 shirt during his unveiling in Los Angeles yesterday Owen Humphreys/PA

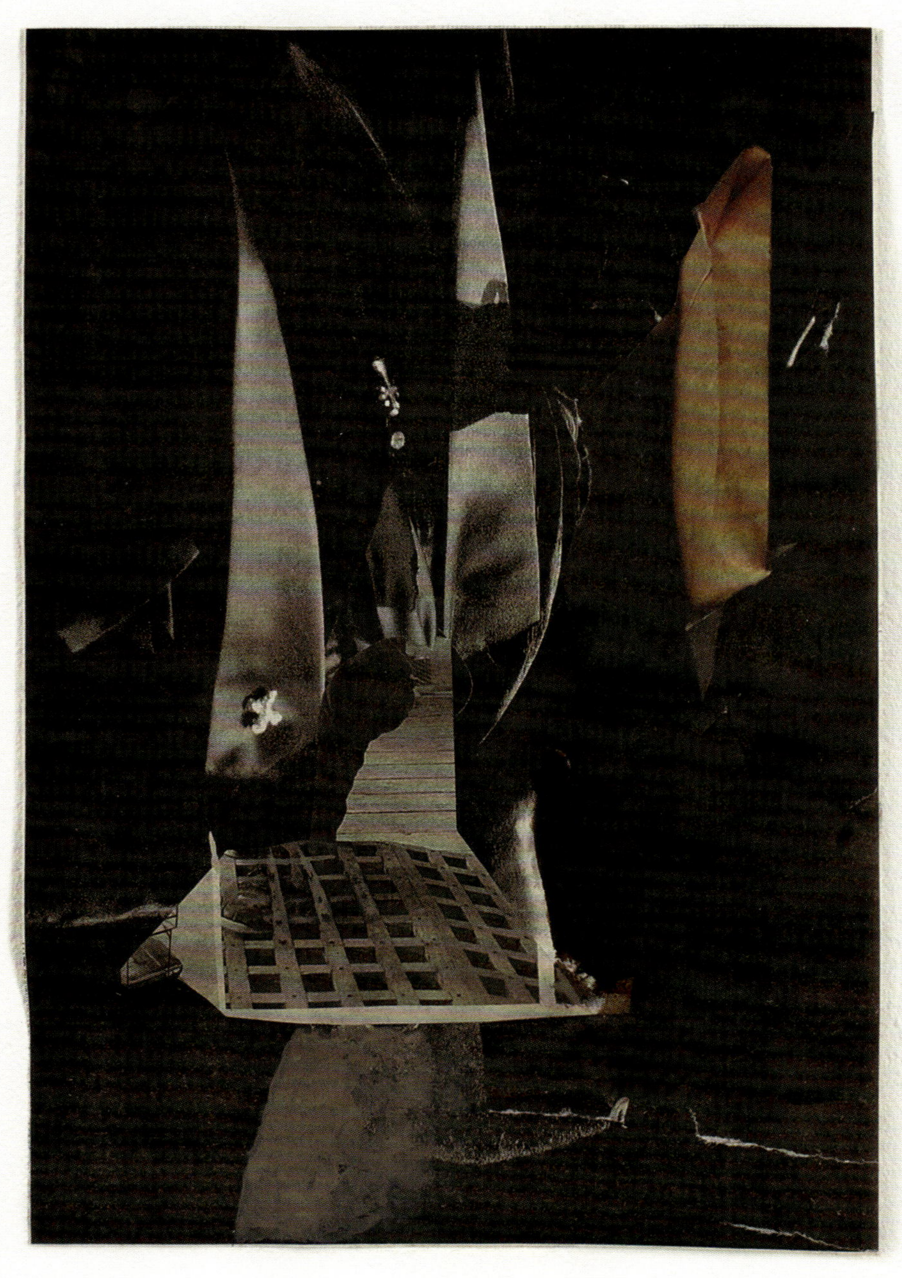

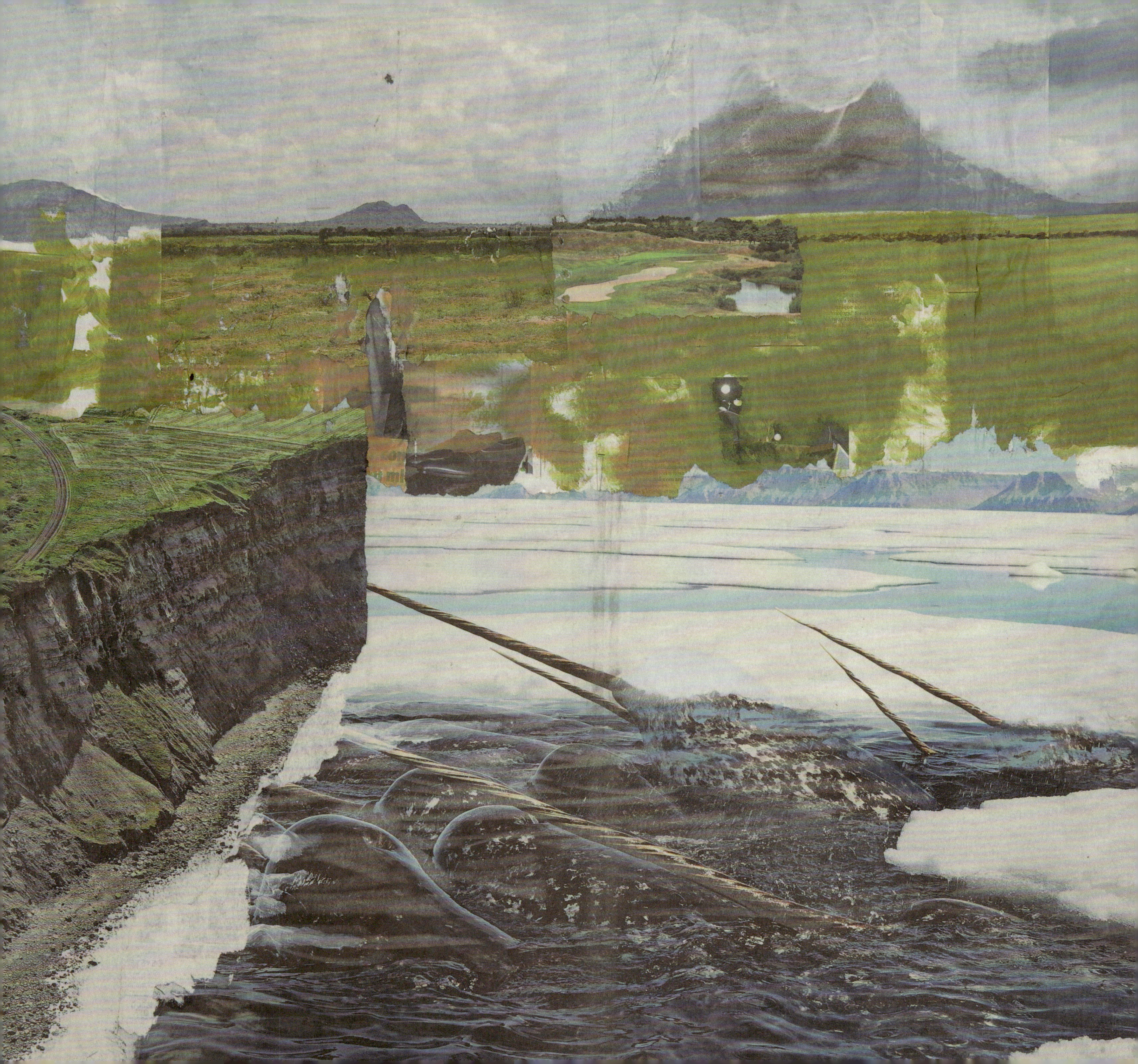

A CONVERSATION BETWEEN TONY SWAIN AND KARLA BLACK

Karla Black: Since there are different techniques involved in making these pictures, all the way from collage – a basic sort of cut and paste technique – through to representational painting, why do you always say they have to be called paintings? What is so important about that?

Tony Swain: I think almost any of these images, that even contain any paint, sort of become paintings. There's different degrees to which they've been worked. In some of them there's very little paint involved, in some of them maybe the original photographic elements haven't been that altered, and in others they have been altered a great deal; but I think that anything that involves any element of paint becomes a painting. The element of paint as original matter speaks about my own priorities. I guess, for me, paint has more gravitas or a higher status than printed matter. One drop of paint completely trounces any amount of printed matter.

So have you chosen painting as a medium in a hierarchical way, like it's the best one? Do you think that?

No I don't think that, but I guess I do think that some mediums have more possibilities within them than others. I think painting seems to be an infinitely malleable, adjustable, flexible kind of way of working, I think that's maybe what initially drew me to it or what's kept me working with it, but I don't think I've chosen it for hierarchical 'prestige-type' reasons.

I suppose that, traditionally, in terms of mediums, at least in the last five hundred years in western culture, painting has been the 'king' and, really, if anything was going to come along and knock it off its perch it was going to be photography. After the Industrial Revolution and the invention of printing presses and newspapers and then photography, people said, for a long time, 'That's the end of painting. These new things usurp it. They do its job better than it ever could'. What you're doing is laying the hierarchical king of mediums over the top of those more mass mediums and saying: no, actually, painting can still do it better. How come you think that painting is better at image-making than photography and print, and why?

I'm not sure whether it's just important that there is some sort of dialogue or response between all of those mediums. I'm working with given imagery to an extent. I'm working with images that have come from something, as you say, mass-produced, mass-printed. I am working within the newspaper format as a starting point, but a lot of what is within that has been influenced by fine art to begin with. Photography and/or advertising have taken a lot of ideas that originated in fine art. I'm not saying that they have necessarily diluted these ideas but they have certainly adapted them. I suppose I'm reinstating these ideas and reinstating fine art, whatever that means. Perhaps I'm reclaiming things.

When you go through the newspaper, you always use the 'Guardian', and you go through it every day looking for something. I suppose you're looking for something good. You see something and maybe you think, 'that's good, I can use that'. It's obvious, in a way, that you must think it's good, but not good enough. What is it about the images you choose to use? What is it you see? What's in the choice to use one thing and not another? What are you looking for when you go through the newspaper?

I don't really know what I'm looking for but it does usually grab me, sometimes its just a pattern, a pattern that comes from a naturalistic setting – like an area of brickwork, those repeated shapes will probably attract my attention, and sometimes it's the quieter moments or peripheral moments that have managed to find their way into the commercial agenda of a newspaper. It's more interesting to me to focus on the background information of a given image, not necessarily what I'm intended to focus my attention on. That appeal is really just a starting point. I'm looking for somewhere to start and somewhere to progress from, and I want to come up with a different kind of outcome than the one I've been presented with.

So are we talking purely aesthetically?

Yes.

So you don't choose a section of newspaper to work with because certain words are on the page, or because there's a person's face on it, or because there's a specific scene. It doesn't seem like there's any narrative value to the choice, instead it's about purely formal aesthetics? The sort of aesthetic values that come out of a love of abstract painting? What kind of painter do you think you are, in terms of traditional differentiations within the medium? What do you aspire to?

I really have just quite basic aspirations. I want to make something that is interesting, pleasing, intriguing, satisfying …

Just visually?

Yes, just visually. My primary concern is to make something that is optically satisfying. Really my concerns are traditional concerns like composition, colour, shape; ways of finding a harmonious or intriguing solution to various visual problems.

But often these days it's a landscape that you're painting, so are your aspirations the same when you do that? The only thing that is the same in all of your paintings is that there aren't any people in them. You don't do figurative paintings or portraits but you do the other traditional genre-type paintings, you do landscape and what could be called still life, and you do abstracts that get really close to being graphic. What's the difference from one to the other, are they the same?

Actually they are the same, and maybe that's kind of interesting? What connects a lot of the paintings is an ambiguity within them about scale. Maybe that isn't so much a feature of the work at the moment but it used to be. It was often hard to tell whether a painting was of a very small set of objects – within domestic scale – that were being looked at very very closely so that they would almost seem to take on the connotations of a landscape, or if it was a painting of something actually large in scale like a landscape. I think that ambiguity about size and scale used to be one of the main features of the work. But I think, now that the paintings have

become more clearly landscape paintings, it's still quite interesting to me that they are composed landscapes. The process is still the same, in that I'm not painting from an actual landscape. I'm concocting landscapes with the same set of considerations with which I would compose any other painting, such as a still life. I have always arranged the components, and now it seems to be that I'm composing and arranging landscapes.

So, how do you do it? How does it differ from a traditional painter who looks at a landscape and copies representationally from that? You are working on something that already exists, a newspaper page or a photograph printed on a newspaper page, so how do you make a painting from that starting point? How does that physically work?

It works, first of all, just from starting. There is no end point in these, I'm trying to follow what I think they want to become. Also, I think I'm generally trying to do as little as possible, although I seldom succeed. I think one of the reasons why I'm reluctant to have these works described as collages is because quite often with the smaller works there is no collage component within them – there is no layering of paper, it is just paint on paper, and generally I try to keep within a given page. I try to find a successful painting within that page, but very often something happens with the work on that first page which will suggest something else or remind me of something else. There are hundreds of these paintings that I will start and not abandon, but put aside until a complimentary image crops up. Sometimes this process goes over months or years, so I just follow an intuitive approach, trying to be attentive to various suggestions.

'Find a painting', that's what you said, and that is quite a specific phrase. It's quite a particular way of going about it. When you said that, I imagined you sort of rifling through some stuff or some papers, trying to 'find' a painting – exploring, physically walking through a landscape or scrabbling in the undergrowth. It's so much of the imagination isn't it? It's so much from the inside out. It's what's inside your head. Well, it's a real interaction between what is in your head and what you're painting on at the time, and there is that back and forth

between what's really there and what is in your imagination. Or what you can then impose on it. You are entering the painting, physically entering the painting to find what is there, or at least entering the page of the newspaper and trying to find the painting in there. I suppose it's interesting for me when you say that because, when I see the finished painting I always feel that I am in it. It's funny, this isn't right, and I don't want this to seem to make less of it, but you can almost imagine a sort of cartoon image of someone shrinking down to a tiny size and then running around the painting. It becomes a graphic experience. It's not that, but it certainly becomes physical. But it's optical, it's a cerebral experience. Although I am looking at it, I am physically in it. When it's a landscape I feel like I am in it, I clamber around amongst rocks and staircases and that's obvious when it's a landscape but when it's abstract it still has that aspect for me, as my eyes move around I'm moving around within it. There is always that landscape element to them, they have levels, they have empty spaces and places for me to go. There is always an agile painterly aesthetic that is open enough to allow the person looking at it to be in it and move around within it. I wonder, if that sense of you entering fully into this imagery you find in the newspapers, and you getting right in amongst it with your imagination to find the painting, and using your imagination to bring that to life, if that personal exploration is an important aspect of your work? As much as you can look at anyone's work and ask how do they see it themselves or how do we define it, who else has done what you do? What is the tradition that it is within? It's not like you're sitting there thinking about Picasso, or intentionally beginning to bring the real world in through collage like Kurt Schwitters picking up tickets from the streets. They are finding things, like you continue to do, but that isn't why you do it, is it? You aren't looking at those progressive developments in painting coming out of Modernism and thinking 'I'll do that'. It would be interesting to hear how you did come to it. After you left art school you did large oil paintings. How did you get from that to where you are now?

I think I had quite a crisis of confidence when I was making the 'observed' paintings. At that point it was completely about looking, it was about trying to replicate or render as accurately as I could what

I thought it was that I was seeing. That was my sole intention. I was being slightly disingenuous – I didn't choose subject matter randomly, but I was picking things up off the street that I thought were intriguing, interesting, and I would paint still lifes of collections of these bits of discarded stuff and bits and pieces. But once I made that initial selection as to what was going into the painting, once I started to work on the painting itself, that was a very rigid, inflexible process. I pretty much knew what the painting would look like before I started. I was trying to execute an idea, render these objects and the light upon them as best or as accurately as I could, there was very little decision making within the actual process and it became incredibly tedious and very difficult. The paintings were taking longer and longer because I found them more and more arduous. There was very little room for me to participate in the process because I was quite slavishly following these tenets that I had established for myself. I had to stop because I couldn't face it anymore. I stopped for around four years. I did a bit of print-making and collage, I made a lot of tape covers, I was always very involved in making things, but I wasn't trying to make 'art' at that stage. When I did get a studio again after a while, I didn't follow those tenets any longer, I was only going to make things that I found gratifying. I made things I wanted to see, so I could use whatever colours I wanted. It was no longer an observational regime which dictated that if the colour was in front of me I had to match it, this wasn't the consideration anymore. At that point those paintings were really about pattern, a lot of colour; they were quite abstract works really, and then I also started painting on newspaper. At that point it was actually for economic reasons. It was a cheap source of paper, also I had left the oil paint behind and moved back to acrylics, something I had used prior to oils. Also, we mentioned the word 'hierarchical' earlier – there is something about oil paint being so expensive that made it almost inhibiting, it almost made me anxious before I had even used it. I was quite consciously using cheap paper and, not that acrylic is cheap, but moving away from oil, trying to use things that would actually defuse the possibility of it becoming too precious. I thought if I had more freedom with the materials, then the imagery would also be freer, so there was an attempt to liberate myself, to break with habits

that, in the end, I'd found quite inhibiting, almost imprisoning.

And so, the paintings you were making then, were they not very good when you got yourself into that prison?

I thought they were good but I just couldn't keep on making them, the only gratification I could get from them was through their completion. I found I wasn't embracing the possibilities of the medium, so, even the happy accidents that would occur within that limited process, I would never go with them, I would obliterate them. Now I feel it's very different from that, I can go anywhere I want with the painting.

So, not much imagination in that old process then, more working to some sort of instruction. Do you think when you free your imagination, you free your creativity, and that in order to really free your creativity you have to trust yourself? And you have to trust your own desire, to trust what you like? If you like certain colours and patterns, for example, and you're allowing yourself to just enjoy those within a sort of unleashed freedom of your own desire, can you then trust that the expression of that authenticity will automatically strike a chord of recognition in other people when they see it? And then there will be more in that for them than in a painting of something that we can all see. It is a kind of surface, lesser human connection, you know, the one that goes: 'can you see that tree?', 'yes I can see that tree', 'does it look like that to you?', 'yes it looks like that to me', 'is it that colour of green?', 'yes'.

I think when I was making the earlier paintings, when I was painting in my most restricted way, the restrictions were partly a result of fears I had about self-indulgence. I was painting in a way that I thought was 'justifiable' and 'viable' and, mistakenly, I thought this was the best way to try and connect to an audience. In retrospect, if I still held those opinions and values, the way my work has developed since wouldn't have been possible. I had imagined a reciprocal relationship between intention and response, and viewed anything outside that linear exchange as contradictory and therefore inadmissible. It seems that the more I have engaged in a process that I used to view as self-indulgent

– painting for my own gratification, using the colours and the shapes I want to see myself – the more popular the work has become.

So, when you say 'self-indulgent', do you mean the more you enjoyed yourself? Or, the more you allowed yourself to use your instincts about what you liked?

That's it – the more aware or in tune I was, the more I knew the process, the more comfortable I became with the process, the more I was aware of its possibilities and used those possibilities, with that ritual it became more personal, quite effortlessly. Whereas I think, before, my efforts had been quite misguided or misdirected.

So do you think about your paintings, traditionally, about how a painting is a window onto another world, and how a person then escapes into that world? Do you think that that is what an image should be for? Why do people want to look at pictures and why do you want to make them?

Initially, it was almost the activity itself, that I needed to be doing something, I needed a focus. The results of the activity were incidental and almost of secondary importance. I'm not sure if the paintings I am making these days are a kind of depiction of activity. They are literally the results of the processes that have led to them, obviously, but I also think they are kind of depictions of those processes, and I am always *in* a painting, whether it looks abstract or not, I'm trying to find my bearings, and in the paintings that are more representational, the landscapes, in those paintings I am trying to make my way around.

And because there are no figures in them and you actively paint out the photos of people in the newspapers, the person in the work when it is being made is you, and the person in the work when it is hanging on the wall is the person looking at it, which means there's room, you're not negotiating yourself around another person ever, it is just you amongst the stuff, whether the 'you' is the artist or the viewer. What about you, do you like looking at paintings that aren't your own paintings?

Yes.

What painters do you really like? I know, for example, when I look at your work I think about Vuillard. The composition, space and the putting together of the forms, and the relationship between bits of paint and half-formed forms and representations of things and empty space makes me think about his work. So what is to be gained, why do we need to look at images and why do we want to look at images?

I don't really know. I'm still quite conflicted about the validity of what I'm doing. In a way it can feel, and perhaps just is, very escapist and I suppose, for example, it is interesting to me that I'm going through topical information, the newspaper, a fairly up-to-date rendering of what's going on in the world – a lot of that imagery is unpleasant, a lot of it is about conflict and the way the world is a bit of a mess. I think there is some of that tone, that register, in the paintings, but I'm also aware that I am perhaps trying to extricate something that is more beautiful than that. Perhaps trying to navigate a way through news events and those priorities and those considerations to this other agenda. I wonder what this other agenda is. Is it transcendence?

But that agenda isn't separate from the news events or reality, or whatever you want to call that, is it? Because you take it all with you. As much as a traditional painting might be a window onto another world, might be a pretty picture, might be an escape, might be made entirely of paint, whether it's representational or not, in a way, totally abstracted, a separate floating entity, the purpose of it, or at least of the paintings you like is to get you out of here, to get you away from where you are and the state things are in. But what's different about what you do is that you take the world with you. You're not fully escaping from it, you're not totally obliterating it. It's much more of a negotiation or a mediation between you and the world and it's like, 'right, let's go over here, but I'm going to take you with me. There is nothing I can do about reality, it's going have to come with me, but at least I can reshape it into something a bit better.' I wonder how much, then, just thinking about that, how much are you looking at image and how much are you looking at reality? How I think of your paintings is material, they're concrete. When I see your paintings on the wall, they are not just

flat, you can't just suspend your disbelief and go purely into the optical, because the painting is on this newspaper page, the paint has soaked into it, it's a beautiful physical thing that has happened to the paper, it's gone a bit wrinkly and there may be rips in it, and it definitely sticks out from the wall. It looks pretty three-dimensional and it is definitely a material entity, so how much, when you're looking at one of your paintings, how much are you looking at image and how much are you looking at material? For instance, when I look at a painting, say a Van Gogh for example, I will go right up to the paint and look at the paint for a while and I'll just be really into the paint, especially if it's on really thick. I can see the behaviour of the marks. So are we looking at both, are we moving between image and material, or do the two merge?

I think you're looking at both and I think that it does merge to varying degrees. I guess I know what you mean. I can be really moved by a surface and I do like to get in very close to paintings as well. I think largely because I have spent a lot of my time that close to a surface, I feel like I know that experience and I know that territory. But I think I tend to start off very close, and then gradually move out from that. In these larger paintings when they are being put together, the same for all of them really, there is, perhaps, a layering of perception. If a painting is really going to work, it needs to work in different ways – it should have an impact if you see it from across the room, you should want to move towards it, it should entice you. Some paintings have an impact from across the room, but as you get closer to them that impact disintegrates, so you start to see things that you regard as flaws or failings, or just disappointments. I think a really good painting or any good work of art should still hold you and shouldn't disintegrate under your gaze no matter how exacting that gaze is. It will grab you from across the room and also grab you if you are 2cm from its surface. It will be in some way satisfying but also elusive.

Karla Black is an artist who lives and works in Glasgow. She makes sculptures that embody painterly processes.

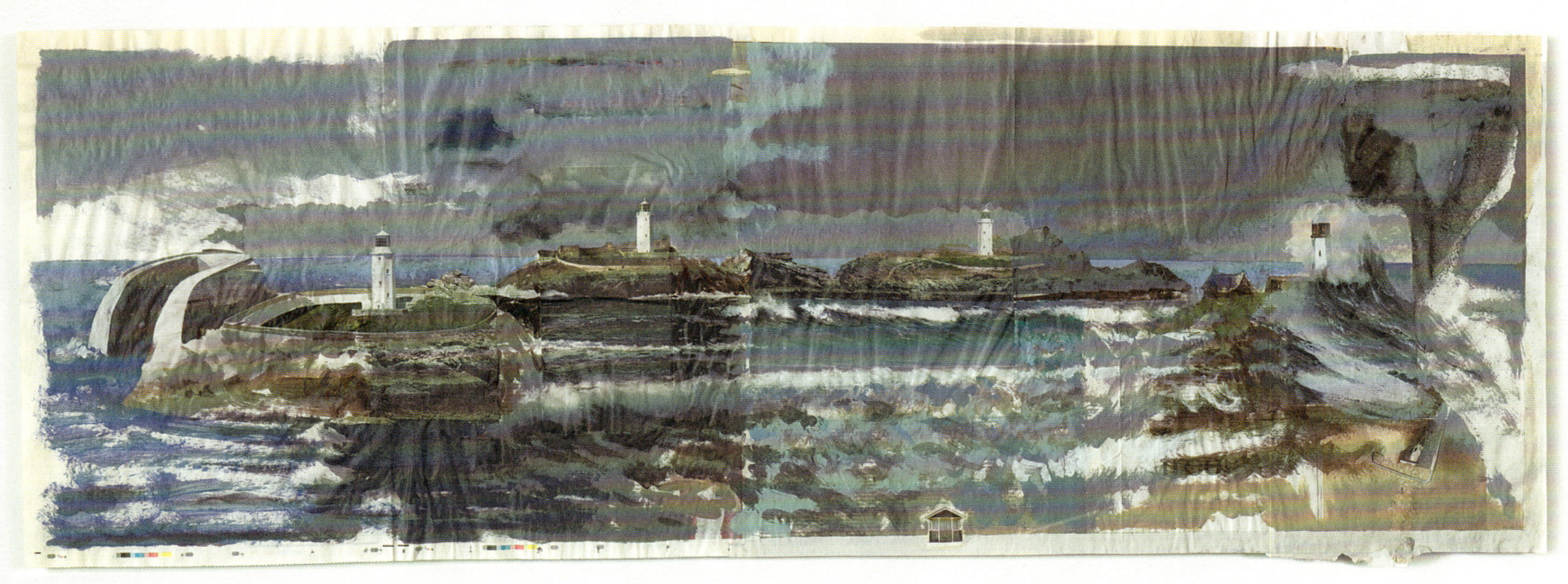

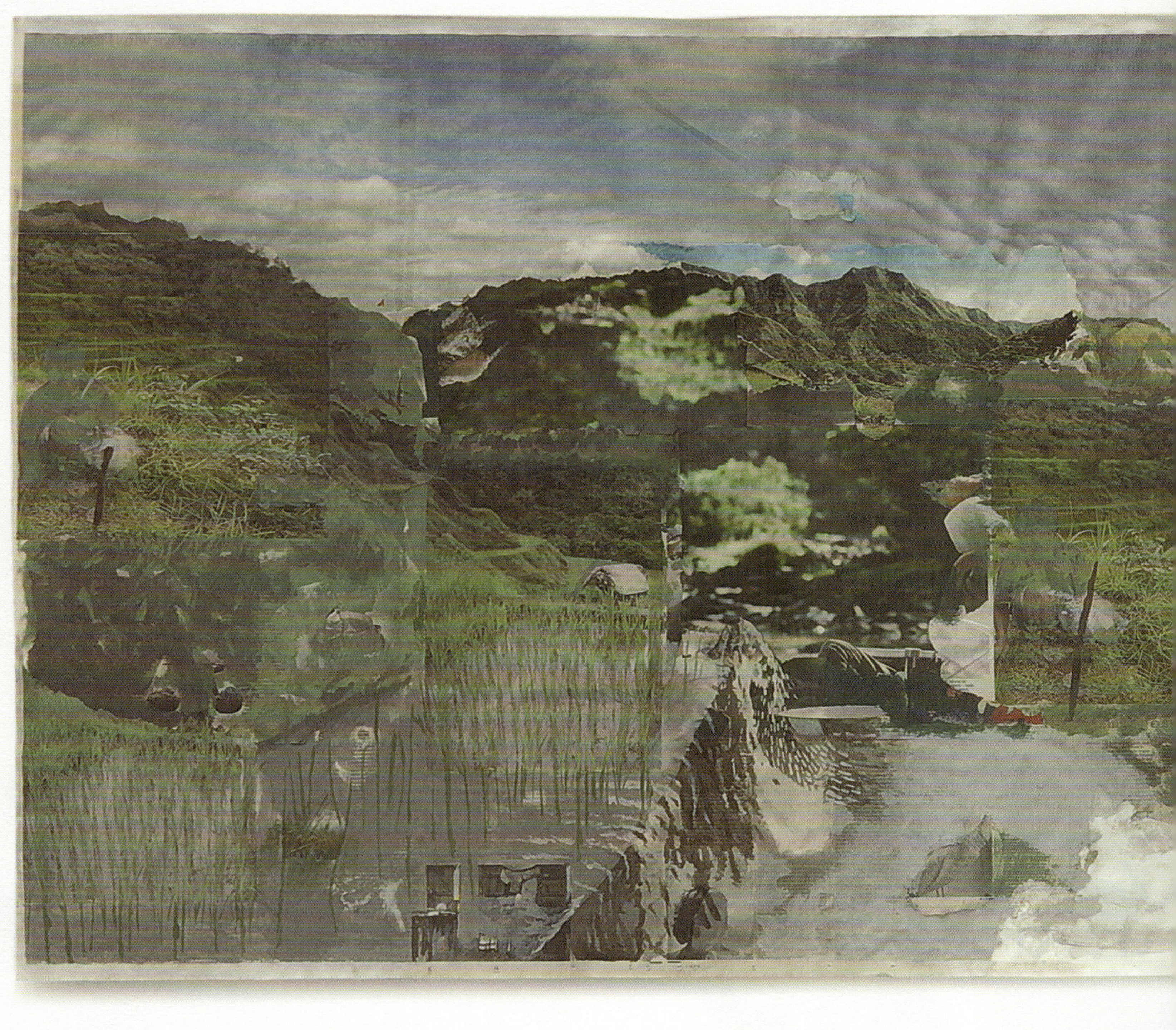

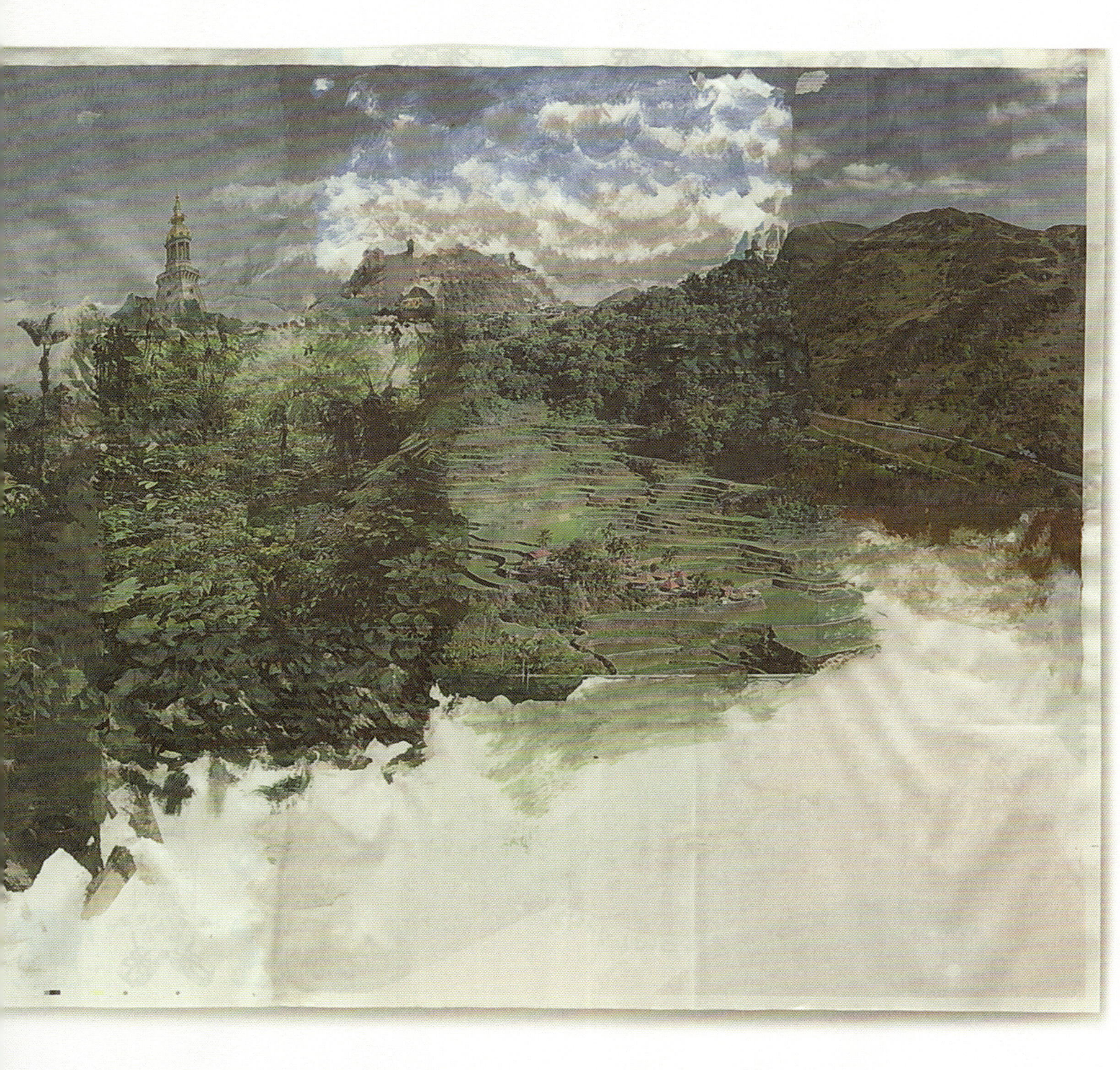

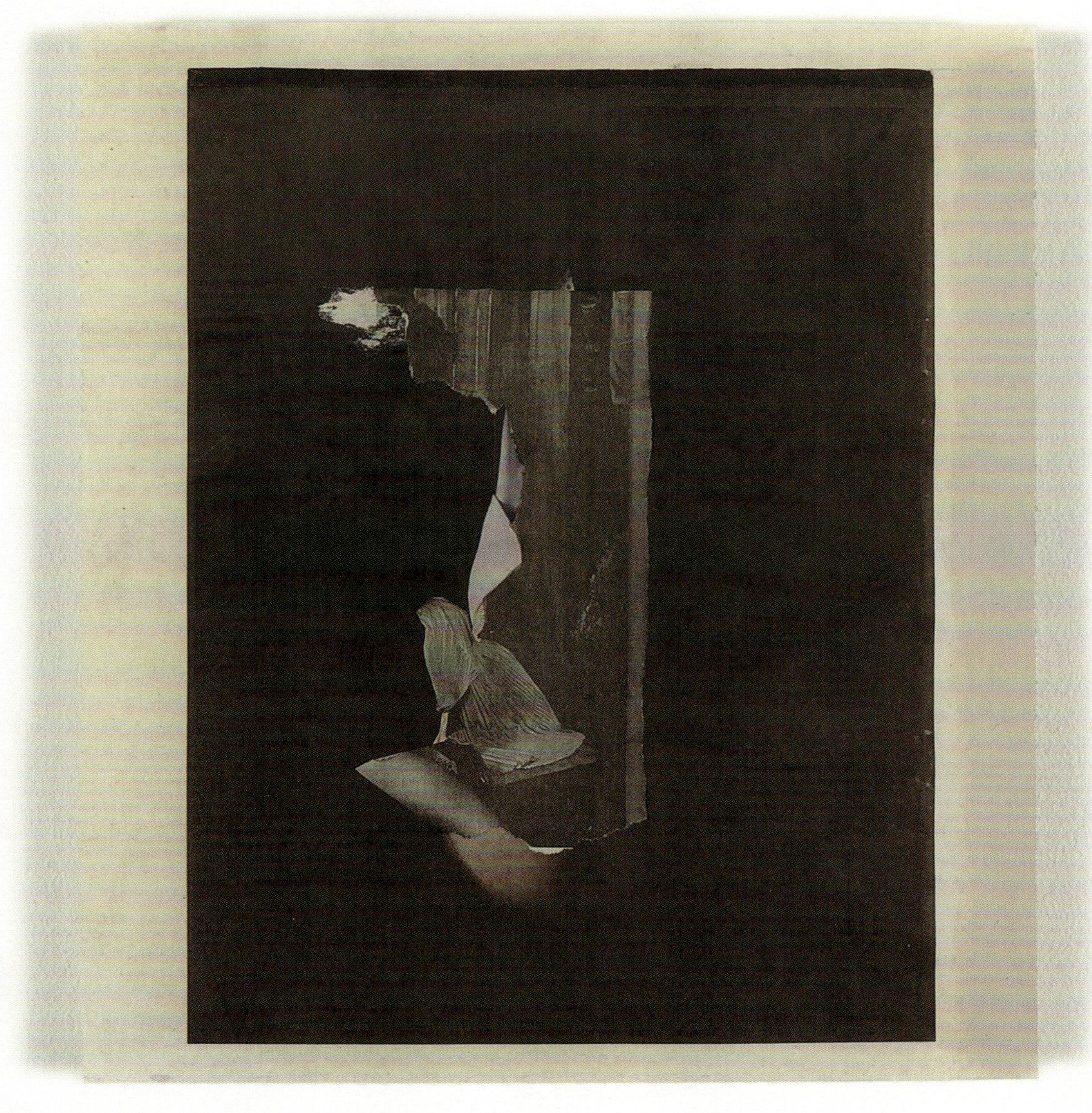

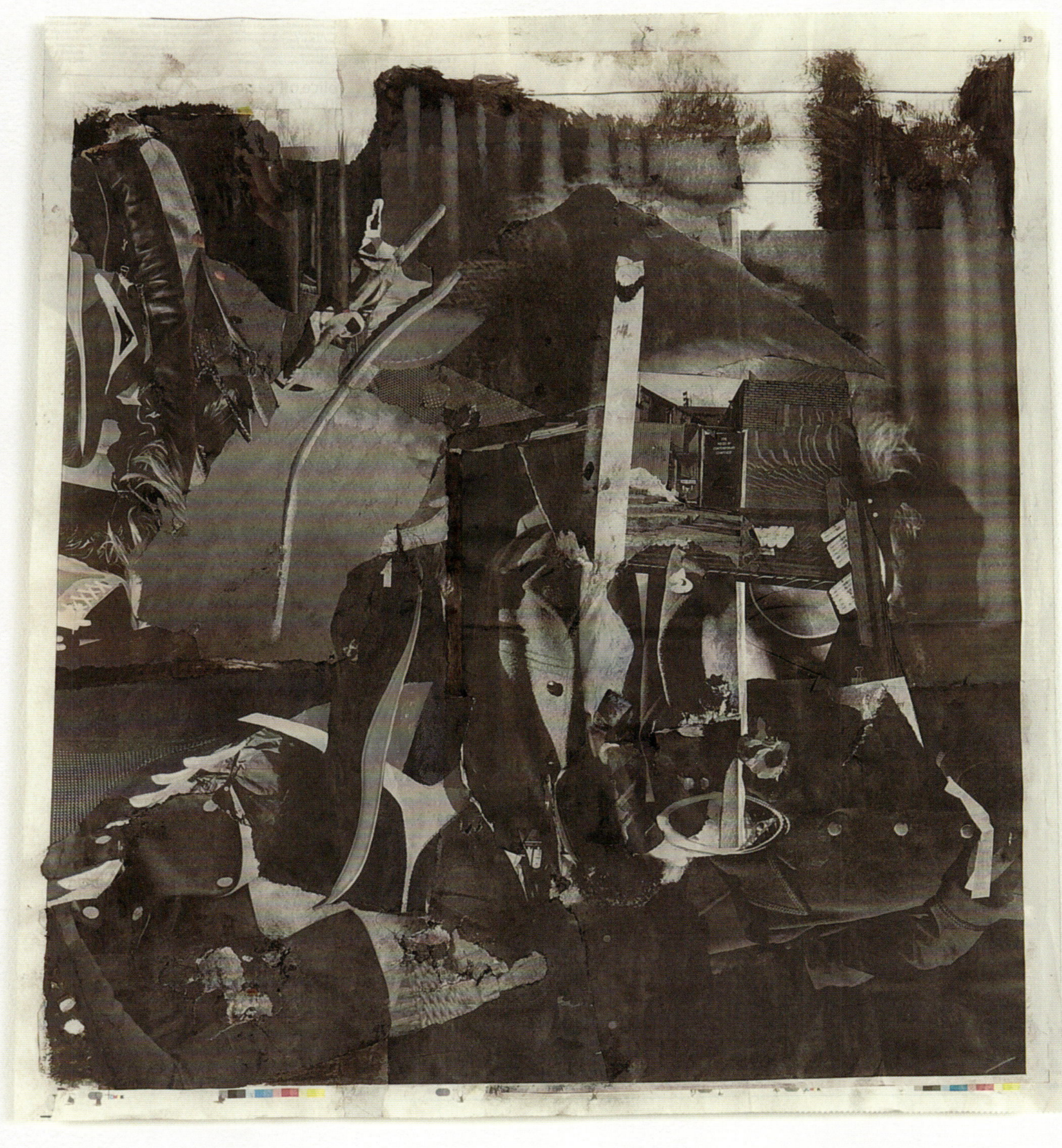

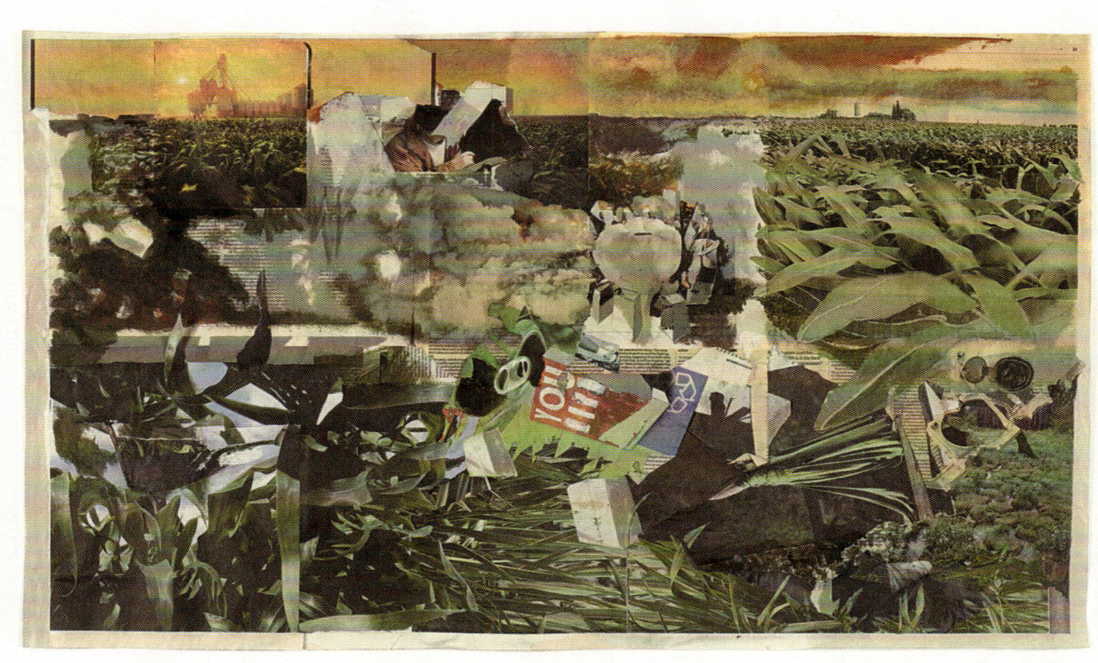

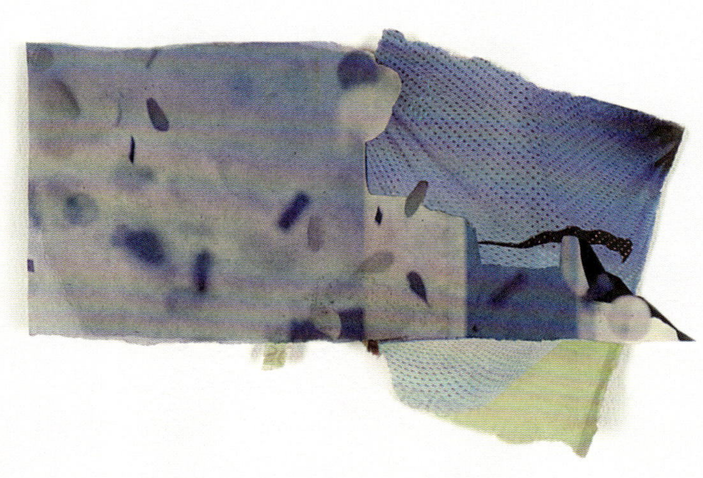

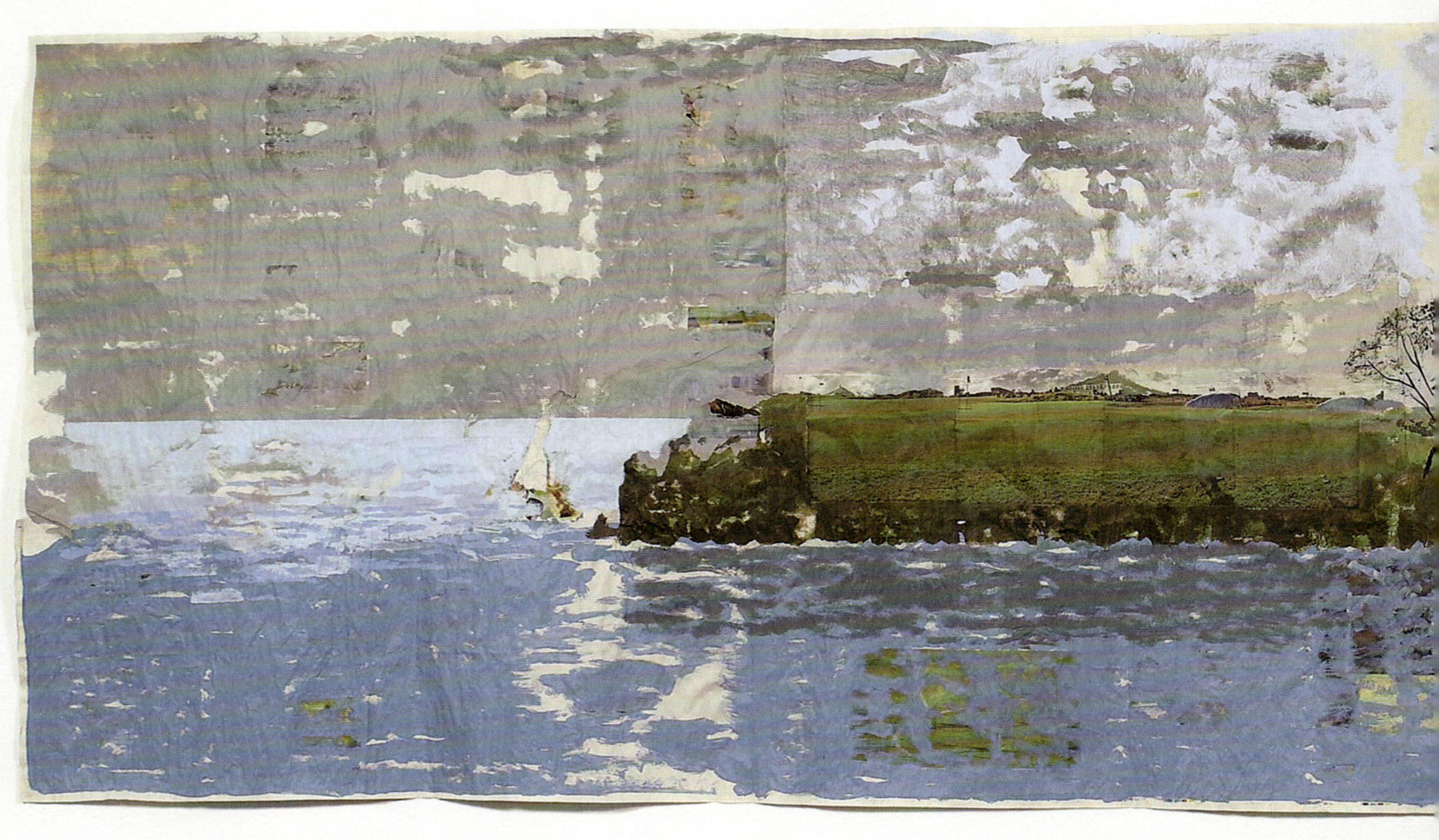

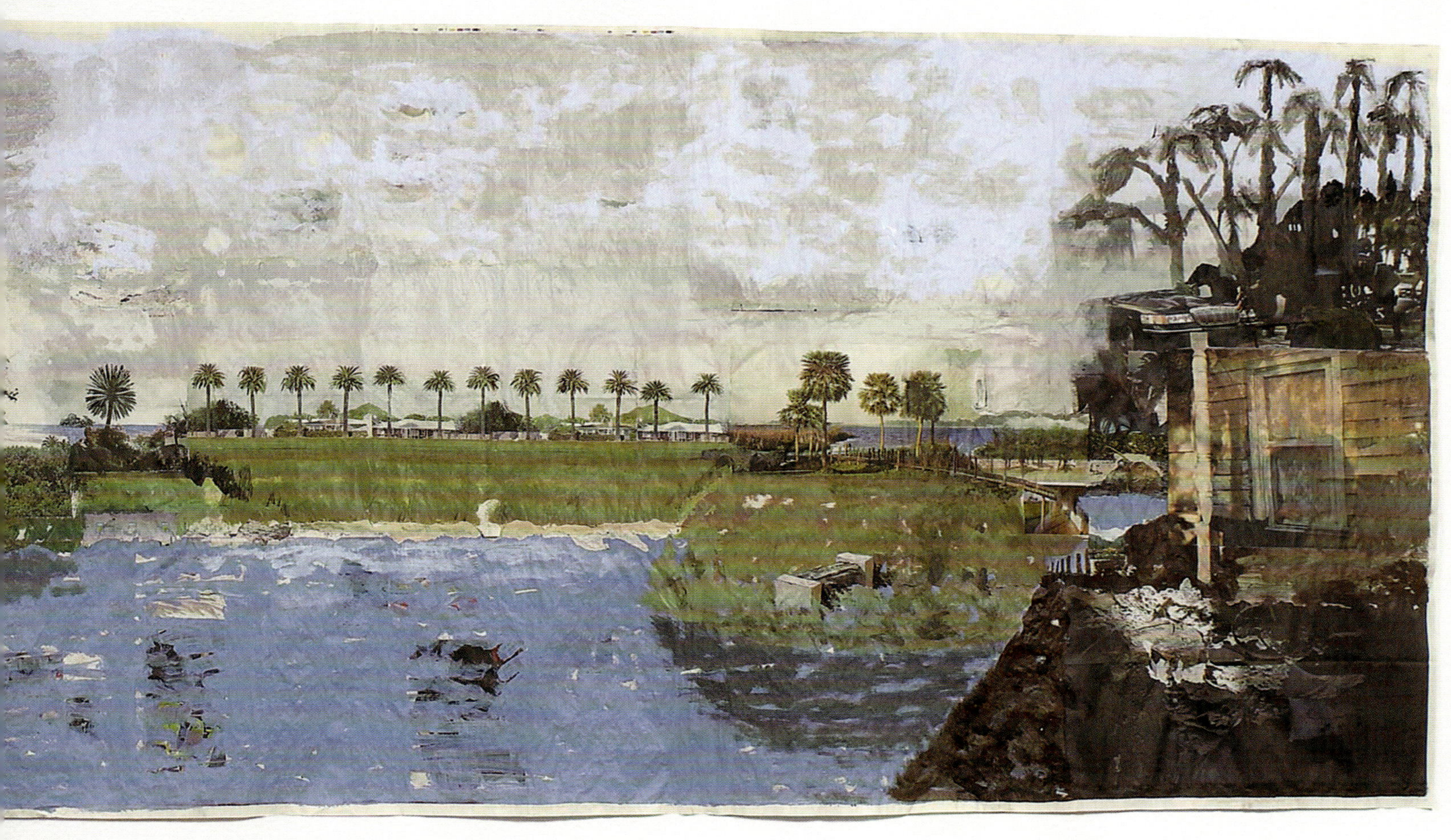

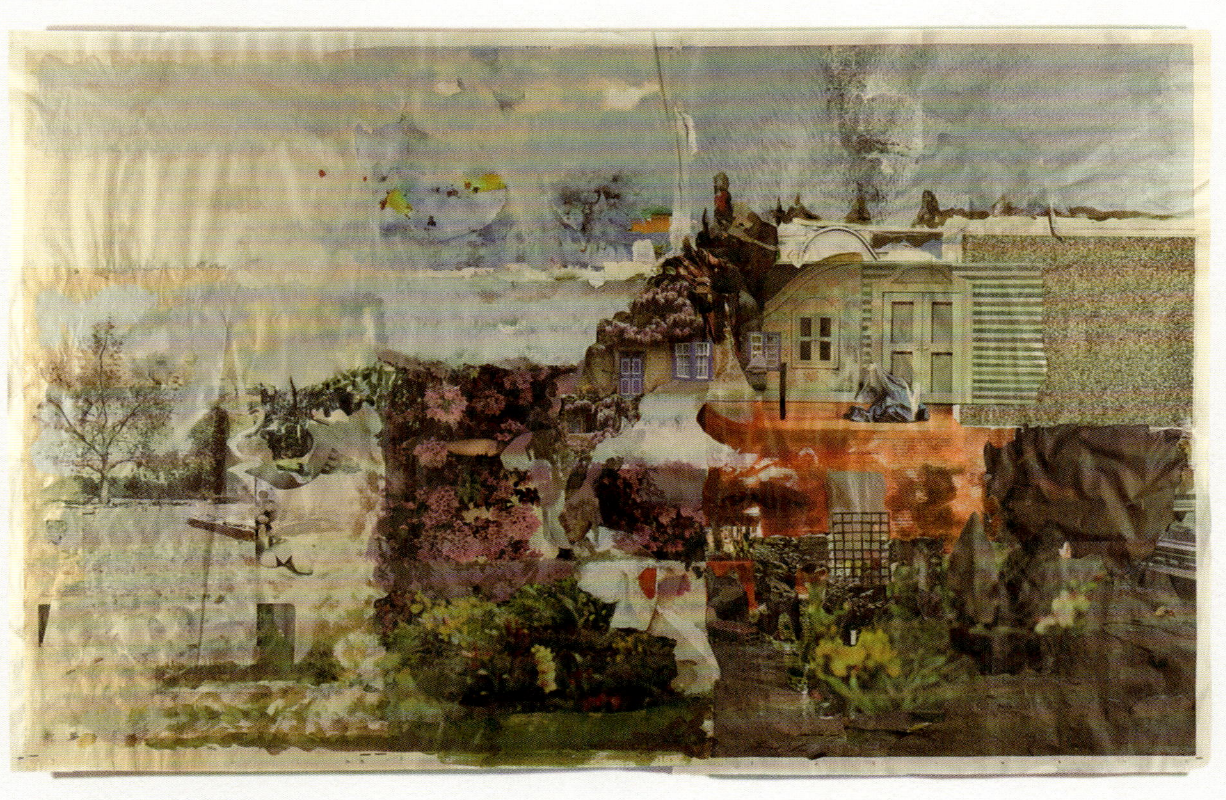

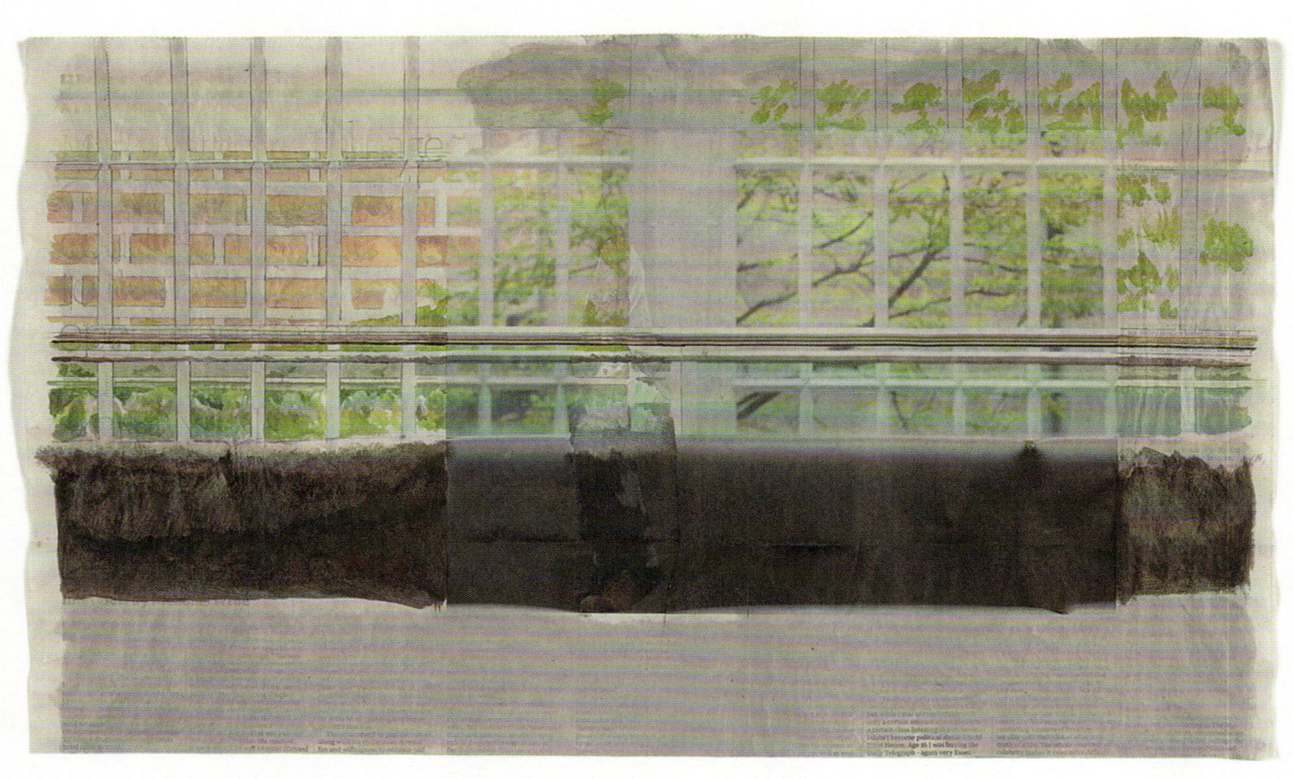

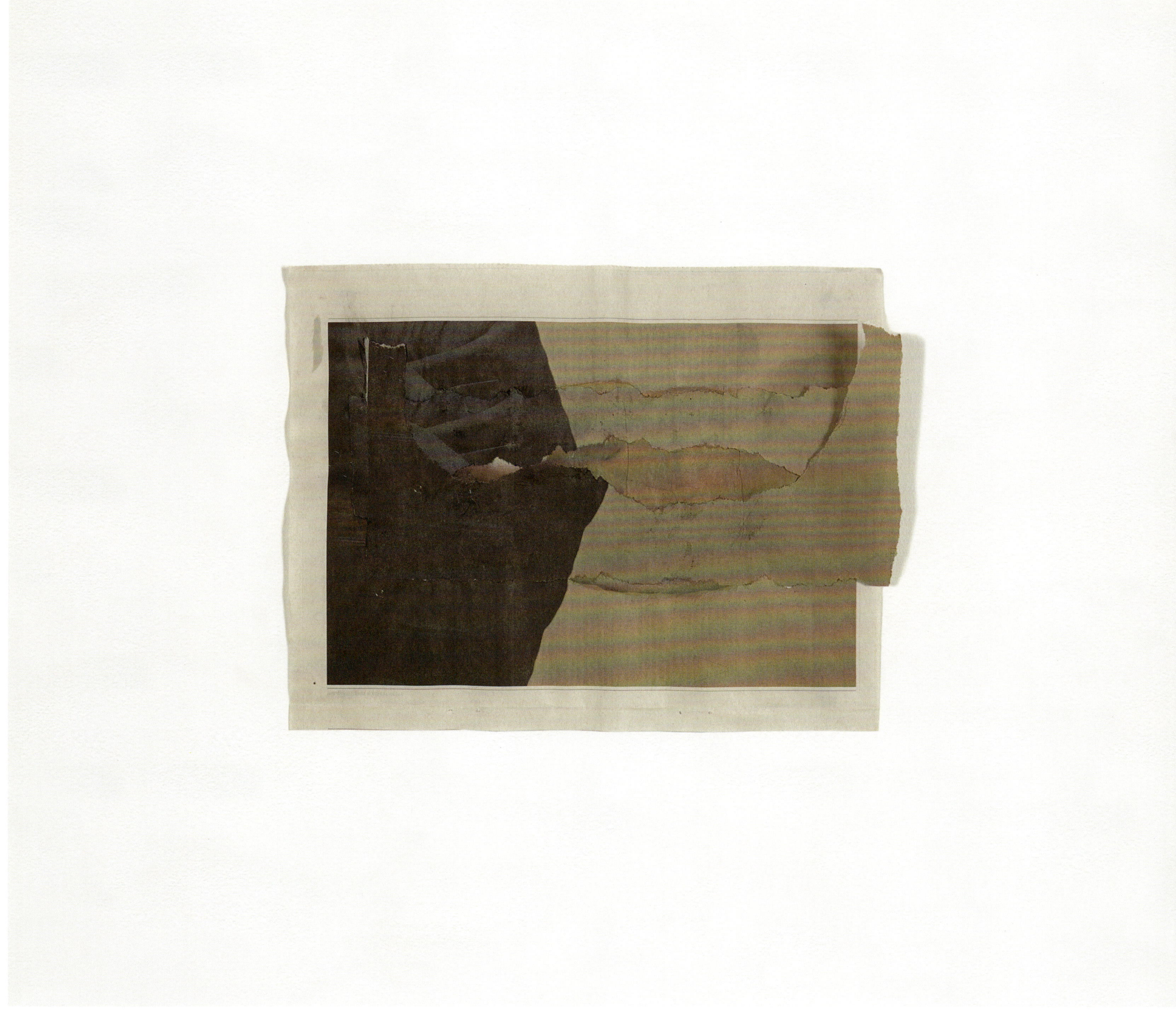

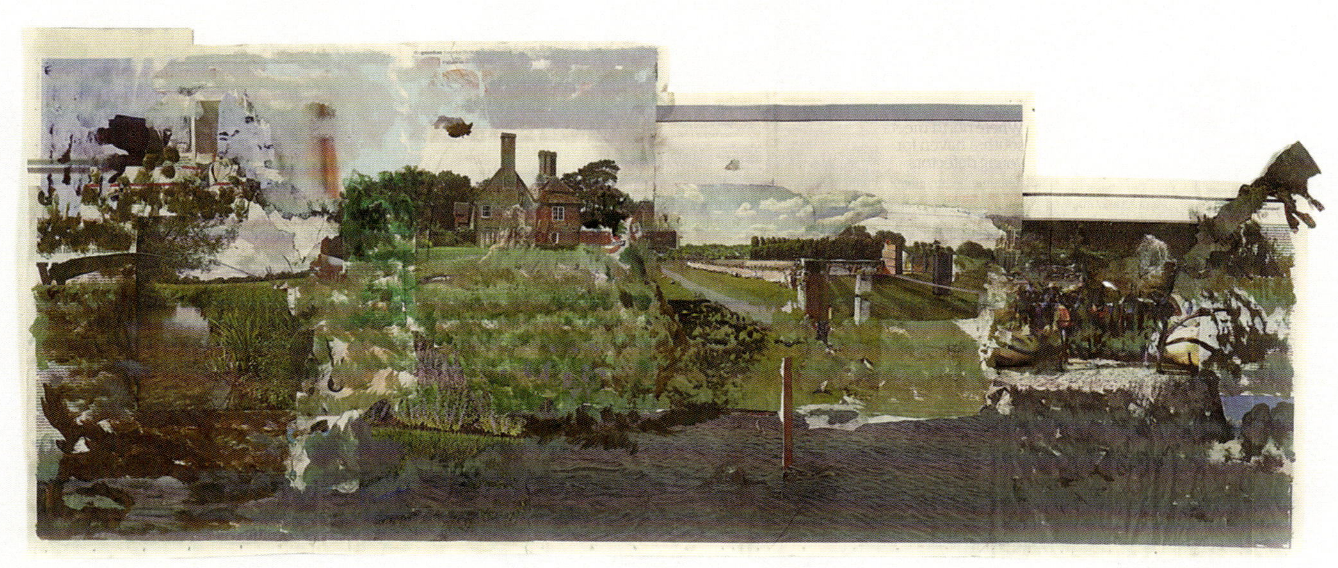

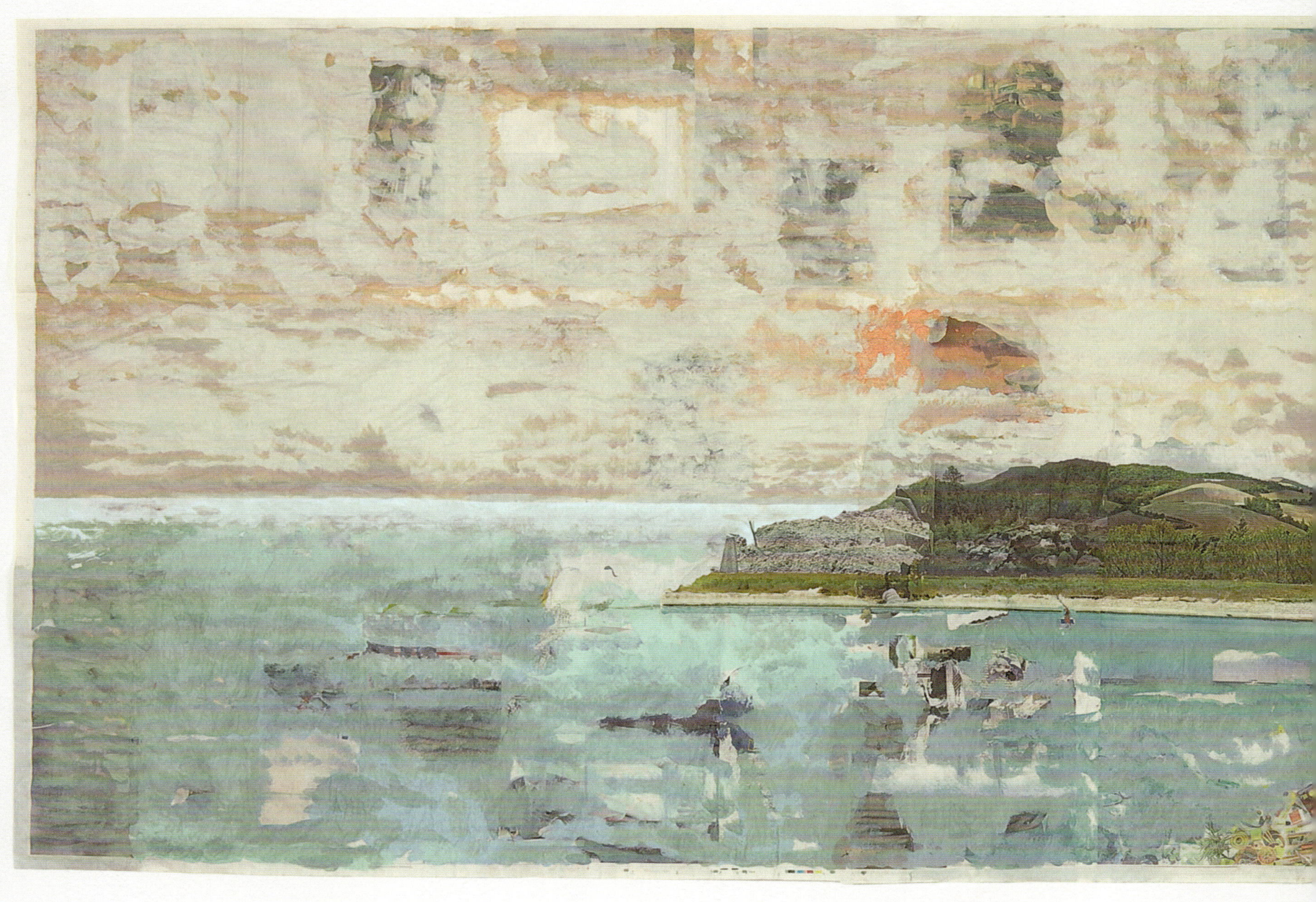

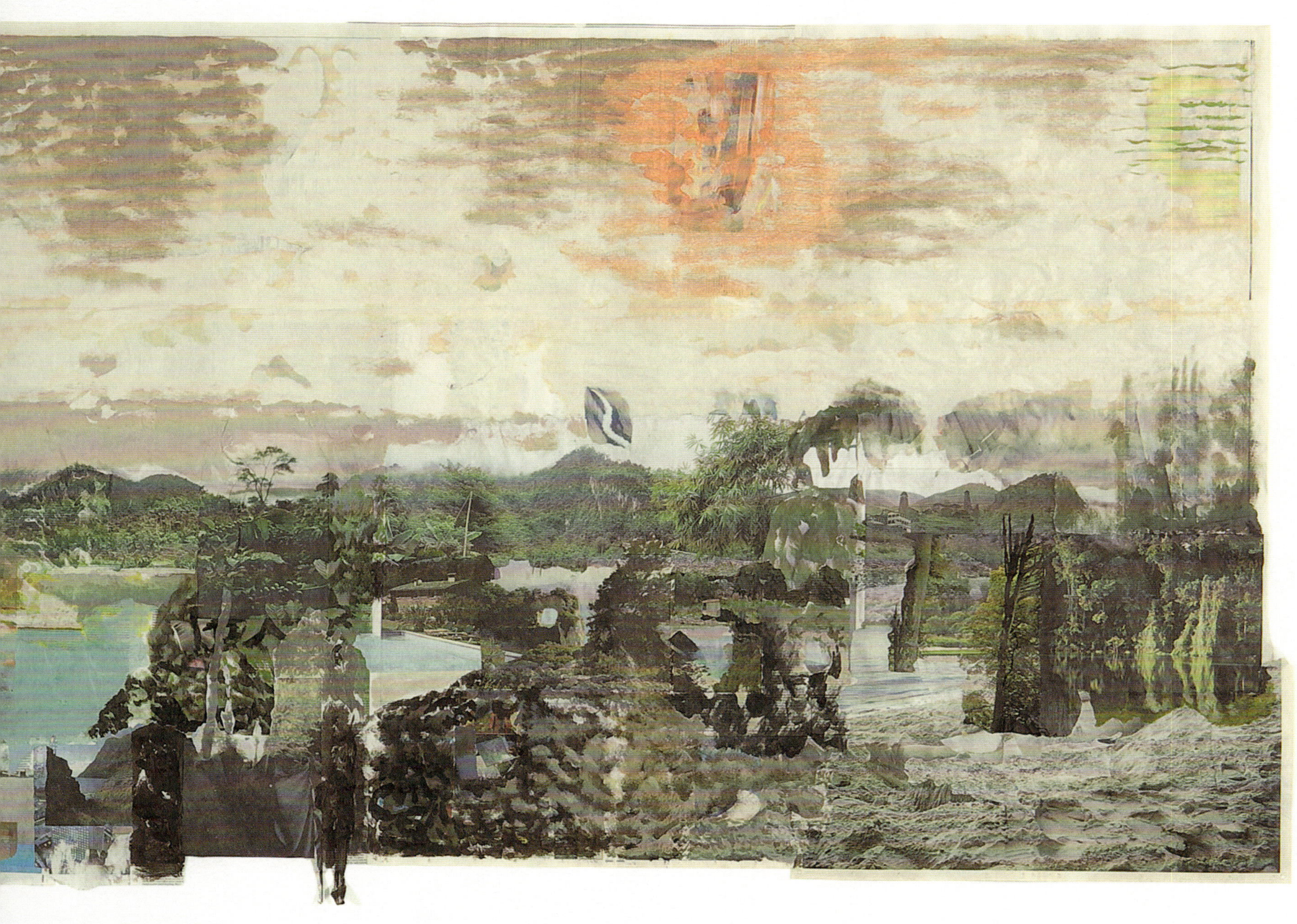

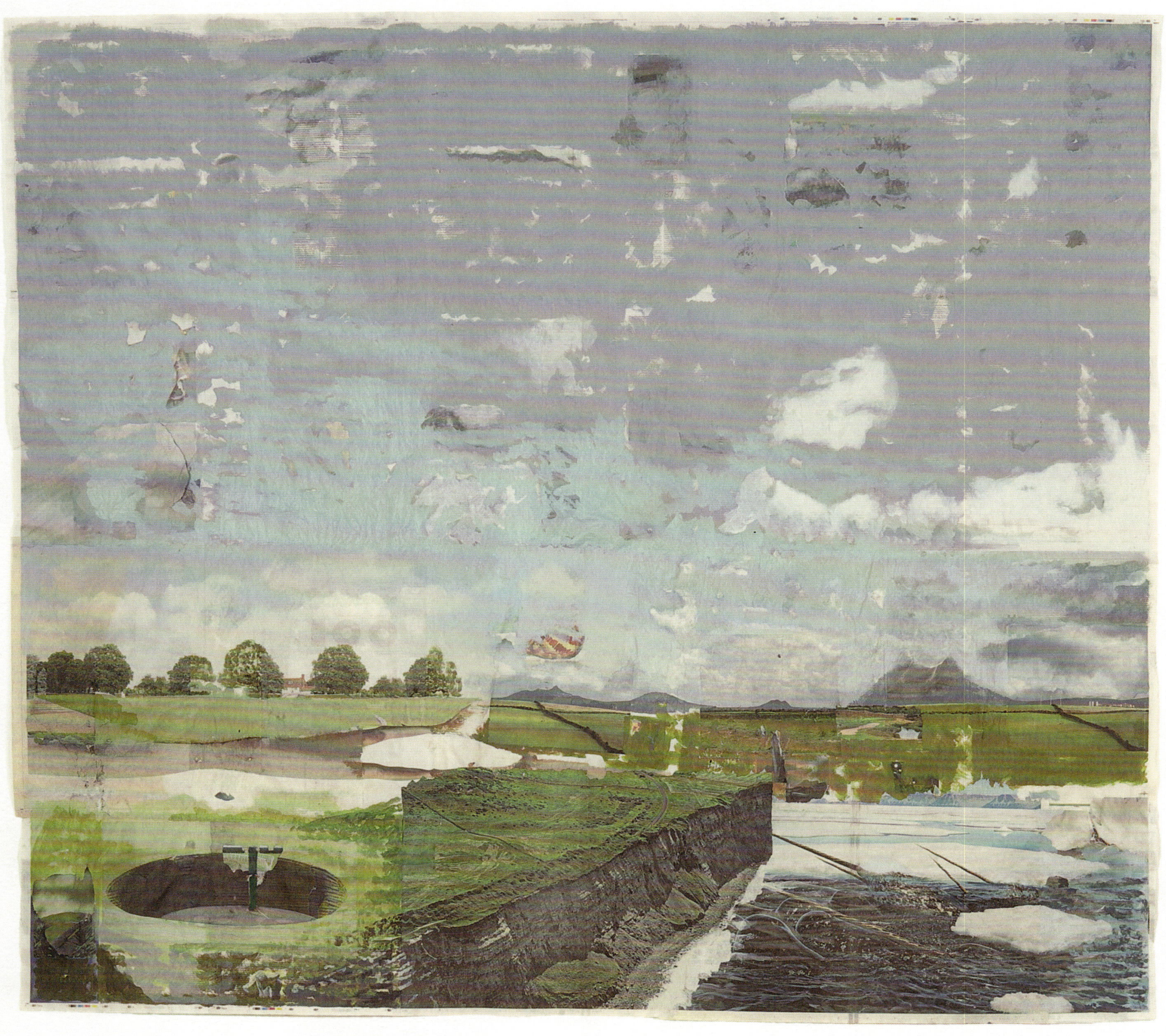

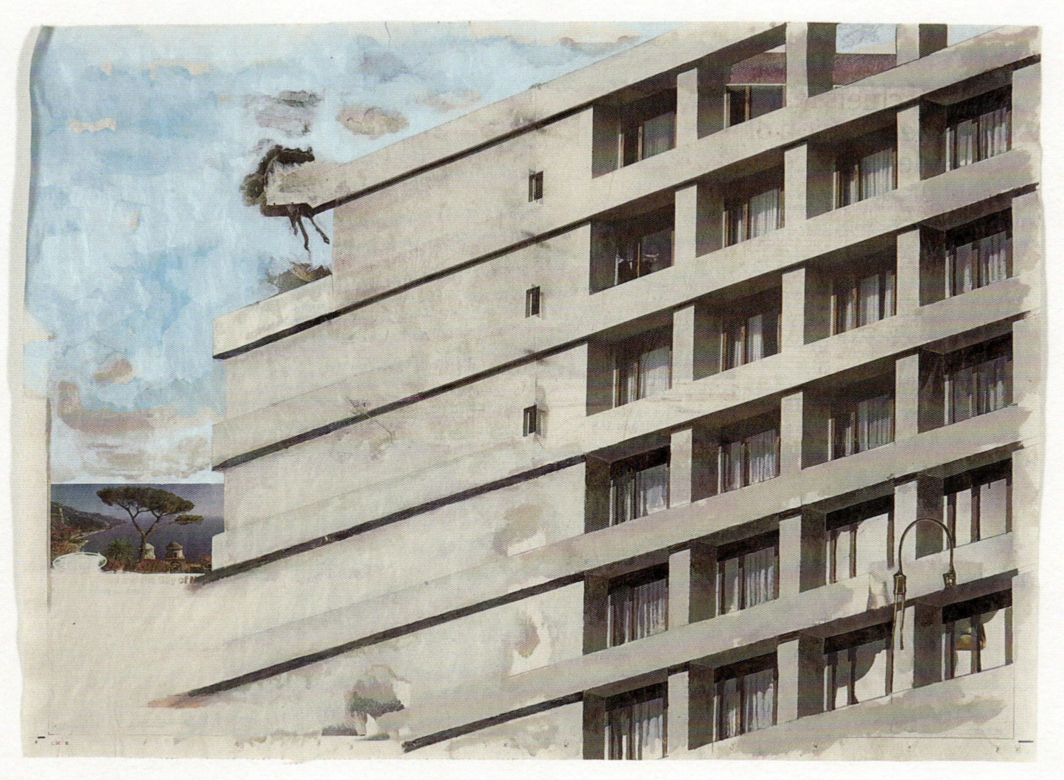

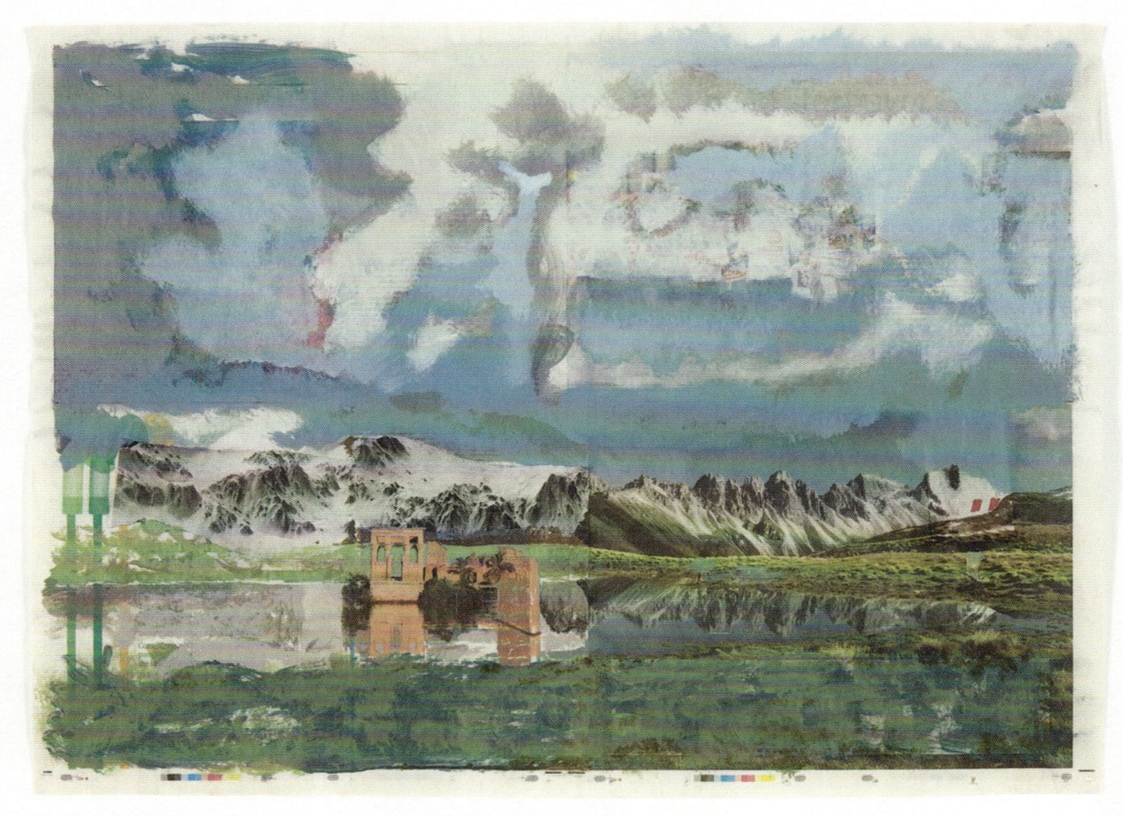

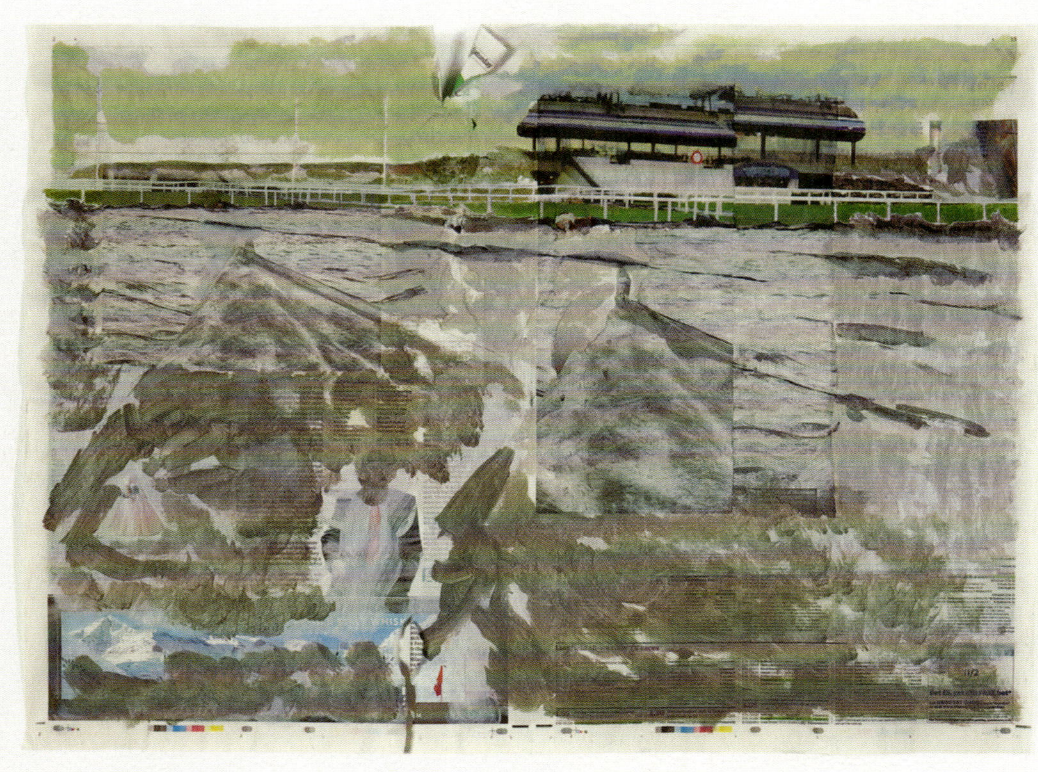

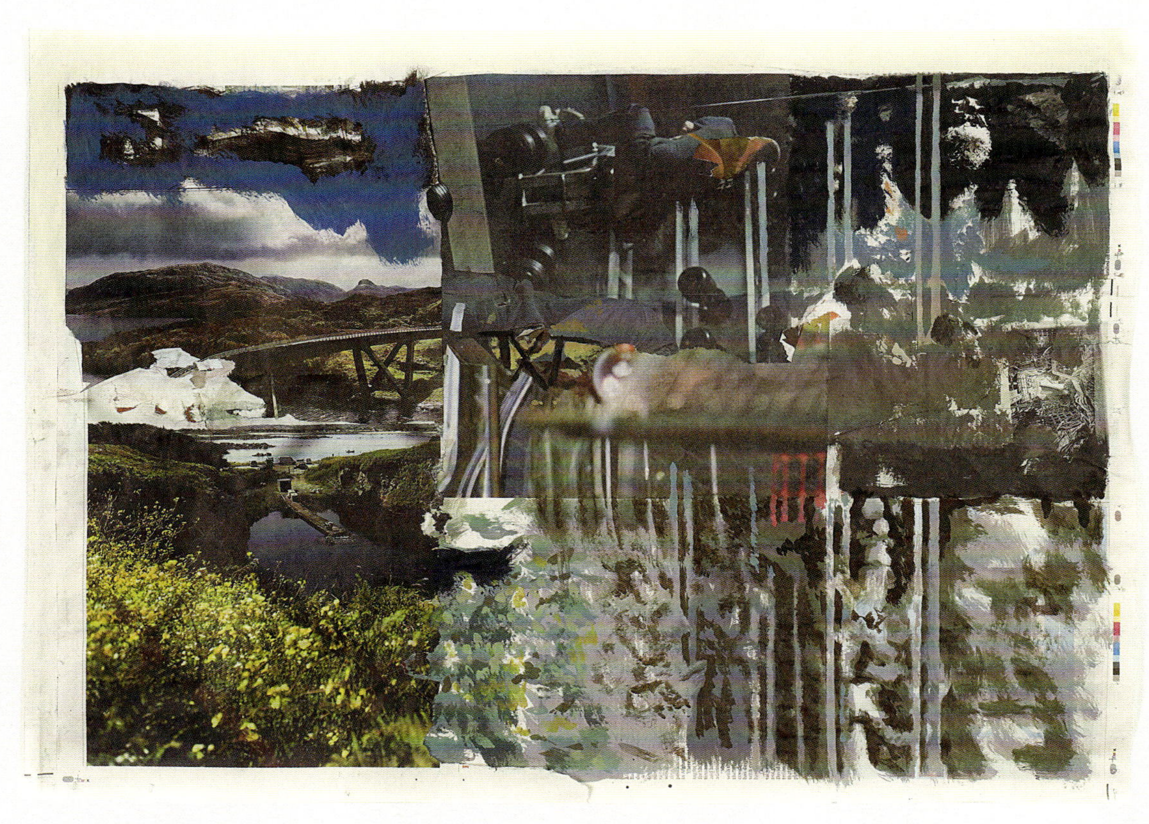

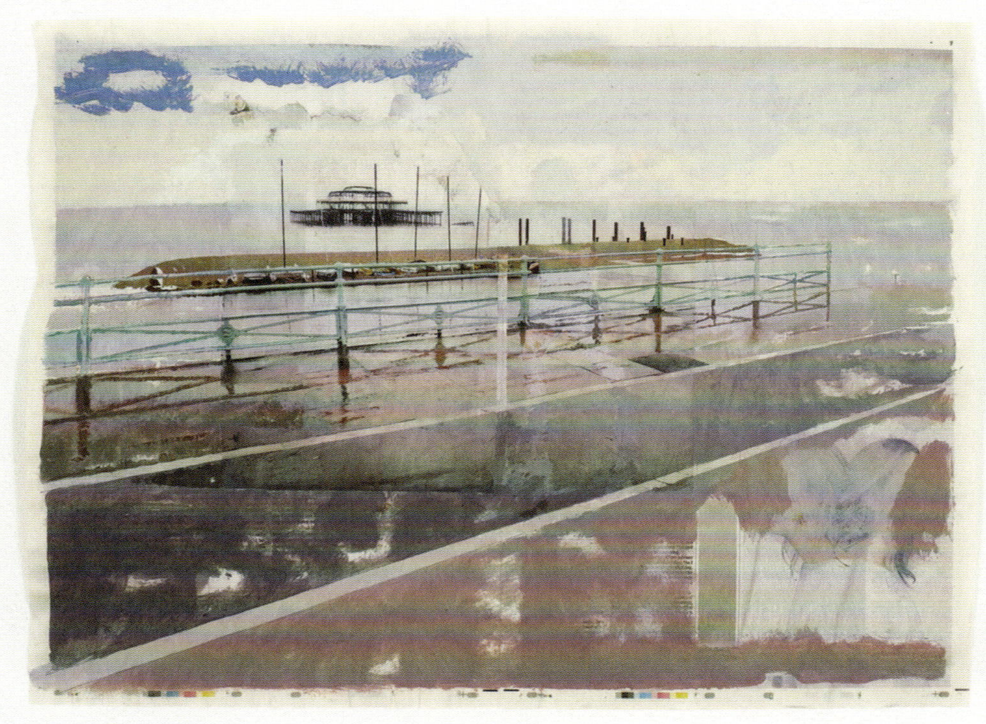

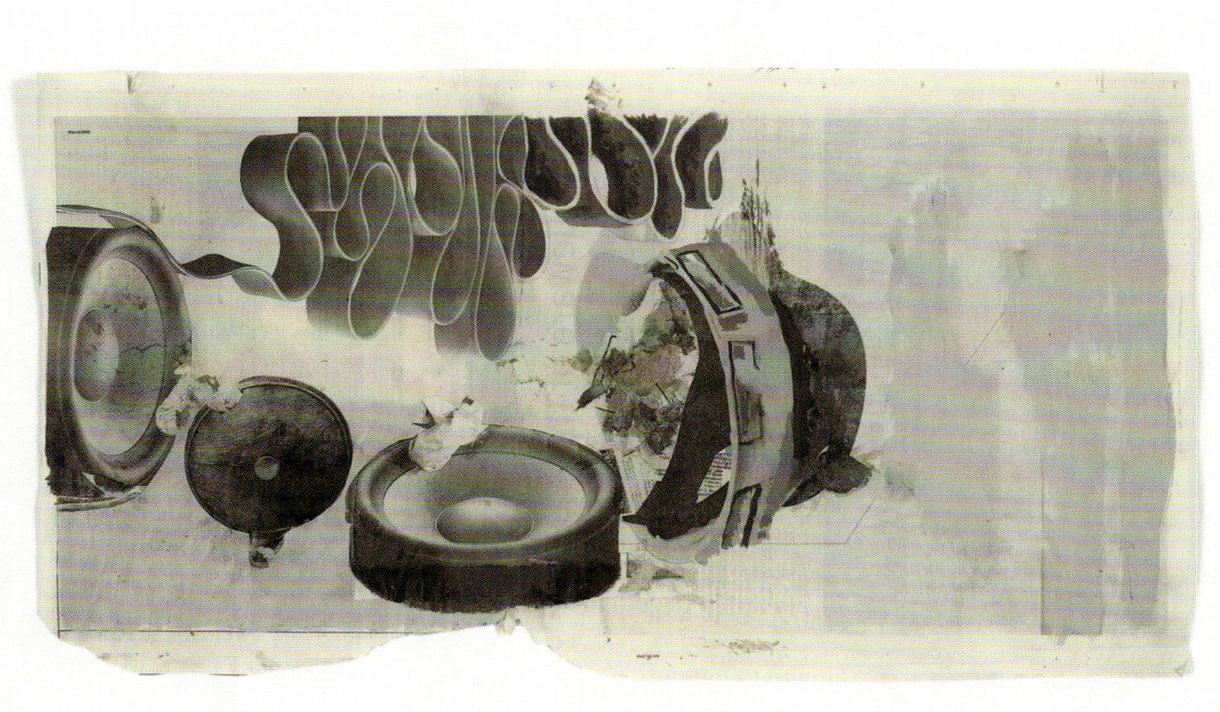

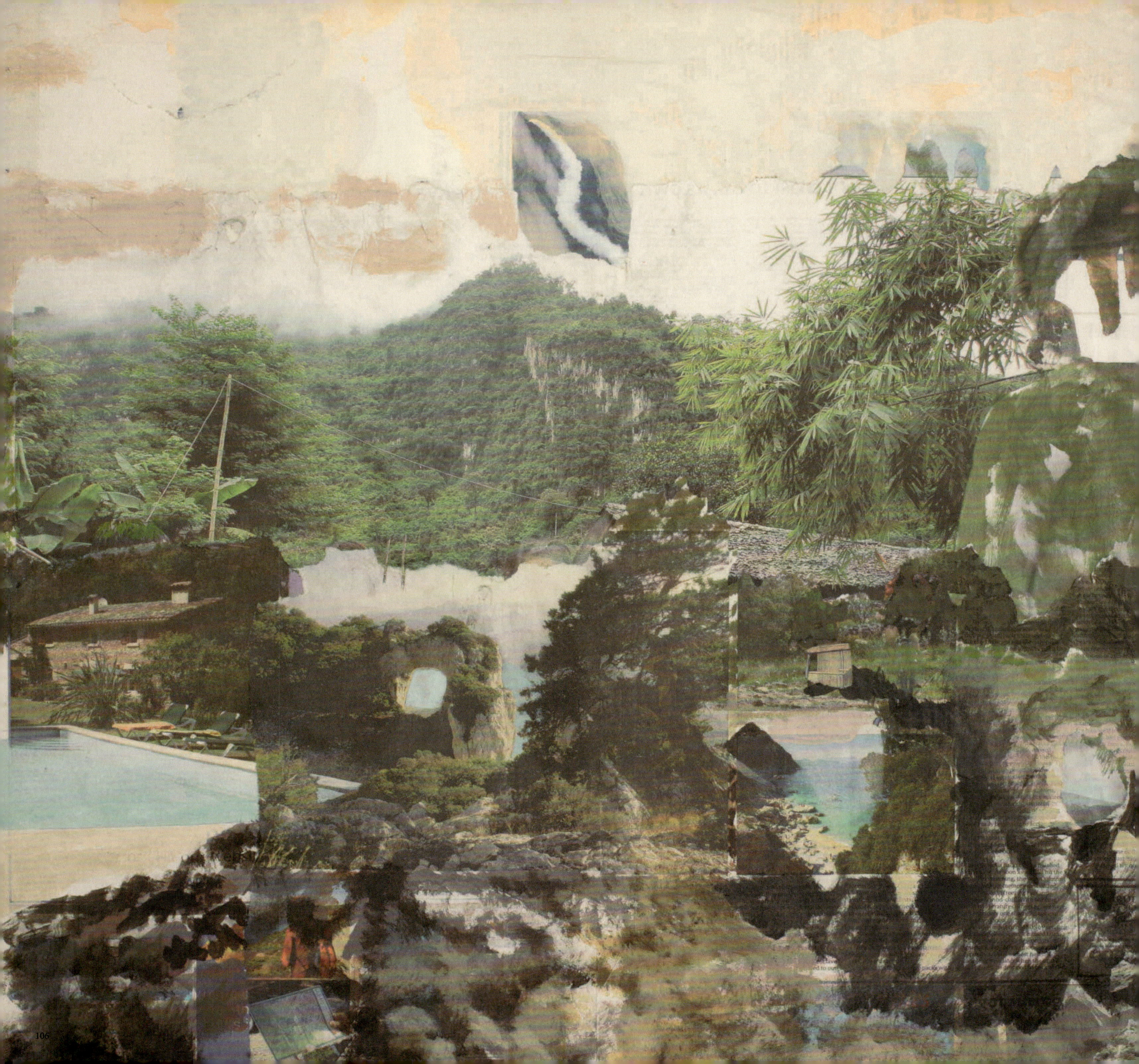

BIOGRAPHY, BIBLIOGRAPHY

Born 1967, Lisburn, Northern Ireland. Lives in Glasgow

Education

1986–1990 BA (Hons) Painting, Glasgow School of Art
1985–1986 Liverpool School of Art

Selected Solo Exhibitions

2012   *Drowned Dust, Sudden Word*, The Fruitmarket Gallery, Edinburgh*
2011   *Afterwards in Pictures*, The Modern Institute/ Toby Webster Ltd, Glasgow
2010   *Recollection Has Not Been Mentioned*, Herald St, London
2009   *Temperature is here too*, Art Now, Tate Britain, London
2008   *Impure Passports*, Inverleith House, Edinburgh
2007   *Soon Divided And So On*, Herald St, London
     To Get Her, Marianne Boesky Gallery, New York
2006   *The Flashes That Came To Stand For Us*, The Modern Institute/Toby Webster Ltd, Glasgow
     Not New, Went On, Millais Gallery, Southampton
2005   *Never Even*, Herald St, London
     You Have Decorated Me The Wrong Colour, Kerlin Gallery, Dublin
2004   *Water Through Window, Husband Mental*, The Modern Institute/Toby Webster Ltd, Glasgow

Selected Group Exhibitions

2011   *Creating the New Century: Contemporary Art from the Dicke Collection*, Dayton Art Institute, Ohio*
     Transmitter/Receiver, mima, Middlesbrough; The Lightbox, Woking; The New Art Gallery Walsall; Usher Gallery, Lincoln; Aberystwyth Arts Centre and Tullie House, Carlisle (Hayward Gallery touring exhibition)
2010   *Restore Us and Regain*, Mackintosh Museum, The Glasgow School of Art
     Le drapeau noir, Glasgow International

     Festival of Visual Art
2009   *Primitif Complique*, Galerie Les Filles du Calvaire, Brussels (curated by Merlin James)
2007   Scotland + Venice at the 52nd Venice Biennale*
     Like Leaves, Tanya Bonakdar Gallery, New York
     Scotland + Venice, Aberdeen Art Gallery
2006   *Down With You*, Bankley Studios & Gallery, Manchester
     FALANSTERIO, Supportico Lopez, Naples
     JaGGy-edge, The Travelling Gallery, Scotland
     Life's a Beach, Sommer Contemporary Art, Tel Aviv
     The Three Cities: Berlin, Milan, London, Anna-Catherina Gebbers, Berlin
2005   *Herald St and The Modern Institute present*, Gavin Brown's enterprise, New York
     Prisms & Shadows, Glasgow Print Studio (curated by Toby Paterson)
     Supernova, Bunkier Sztuki, Krakow (British Council touring exhibition)*
2004   Transmission, Glasgow
     Kerlin Gallery, Dublin
     Glasgow Art Fair (with Switchspace)
     Curb Your Enthusiasm, Millers Terrace, London

Selected Publications

2011   *Creating the New Century: Contemporary Art from the Dicke Collection*, The Dayton Art Institute, Ohio
2008   *Tony Swain: Paintings*, DuMont Buchverlag, Cologne
     Scotland + Venice 2003 2005 2007, Fiona Bradley (ed.), Scottish Arts Council, Edinburgh
2005   *Supernova*, British Council, London

Selected Articles

2010   Cooper, Neil, 'Tommy Grace, Ged Quinn and Tony Swain: Restore Us and Regain', *The List*, Issue 670
     Macmillan, Duncan, 'Art: Lessons from a past master on making a good impression', *The Scotsman*, 21 October
     'topsy turvy', *The Big Issue*, 27 September

2009   Swain, Tony, 'Tony Swain on how he paints', *Observer*, 20 September
     'Tate Britain presents new paintings by Glasgow-based artist Tony Swain', *Art Knowledge News*, 26 June
     Coomer, Martin, 'News Style', *The Big Issue*, May
2008   Black, Karla, 'Extract from "This Is A Ticket" in Tony Swain/Paintings', *The New Paper*, August
     Lesso, Rosie, 'Nick Evans and Tony Swain', *The List*, Issue 597
     Kennedy, Alexander, 'Nick Evans and Tony Swain', *The List*, Issue 597
2007   Leaver-Yap, Isla, 'Art and mud: Venice Biennale', *The List*, Issue 578
     Leaver-Yap, Isla, 'Concrete Planes', *Map*, Issue 11
2006   Anderson, Randall, 'Tony Swain', *Flash Art*, No. 250
     Peter, Mick, 'Tony Swain', *frieze*, Issue 102
     Kennedy, Alexander, 'Tony Swain: The Flashes that Came to Stand For Us', *The List*, July
     Harrison, Sara, 'Tony Swain', *Art Monthly*, February
     Sumpter, Helen, 'Tony Swain', *Time Out London*, January
2004   McDermott, Leon, 'Tony Swain', *The Metro*, 17 September
     Jeffrey, Moira, 'Showing vital spark', *The Herald*, 10 September
     McLaughlin, Aideen, 'Writings on the Wall', *The Big Issue*, September
     James, Merlin, 'Munro, Pollard and Swain at Transmission', *Transmission Newsletter*, April
     Figgis, Laurence, 'JP Munro, Alex Pollard, Tony Swain', *Untitled*, October
     Price, Matt, 'Tony Swain, in Mixed Paint: A survey of contemporary painters', *Flash Art*, No. 239

---

* Denotes catalogue

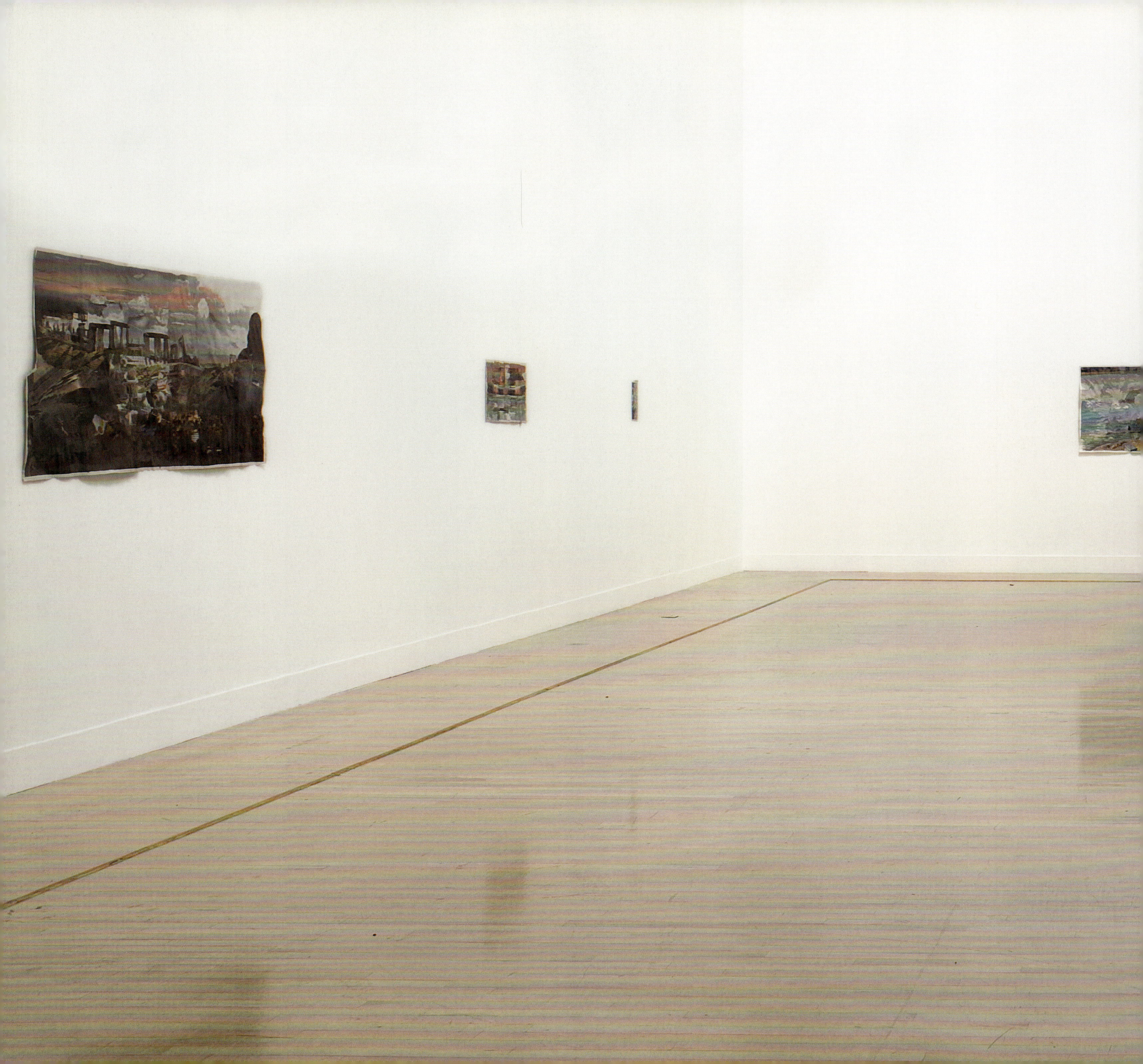

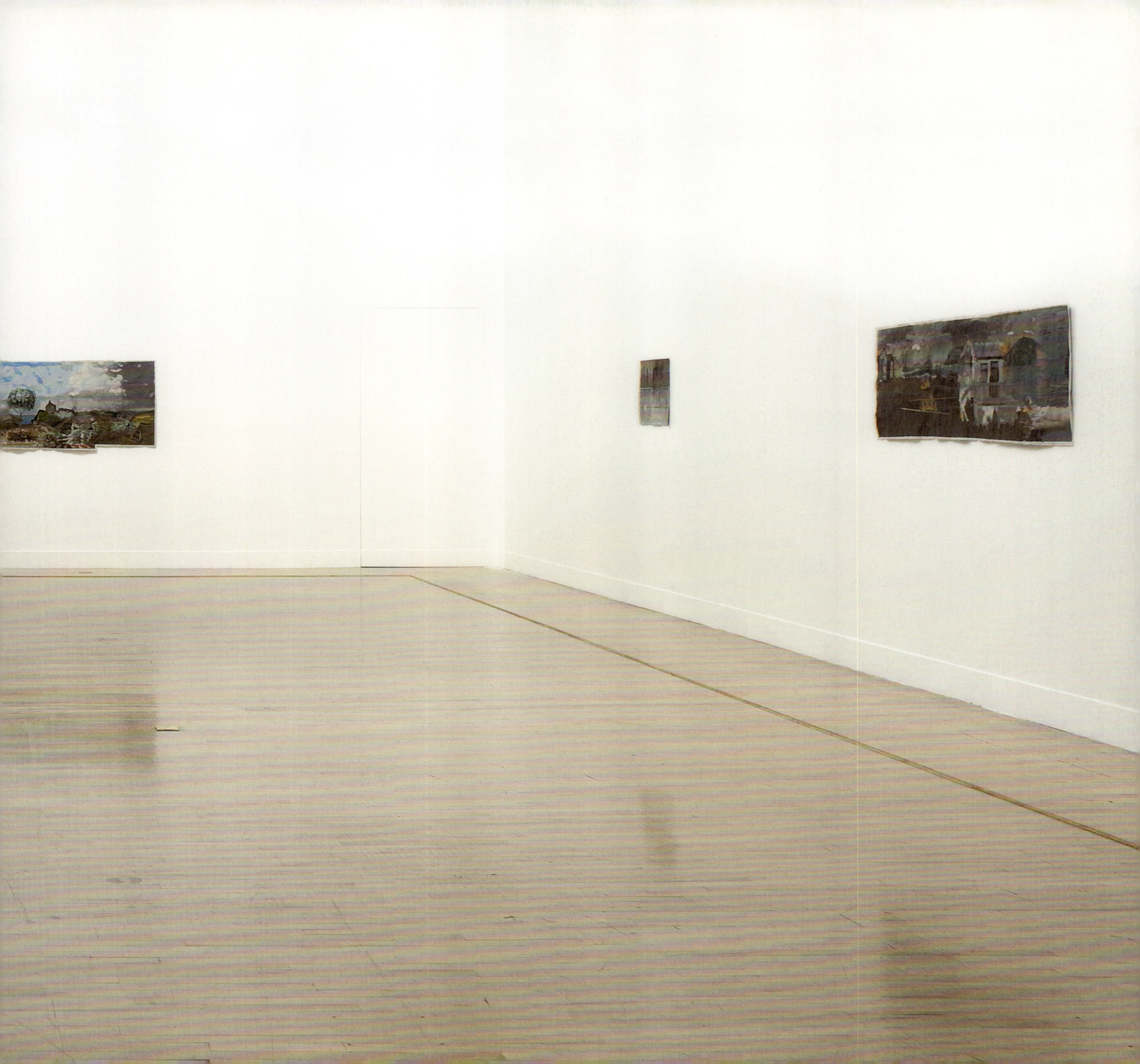

PLATE LIST

p.5
Idle as totems, 2012
Acrylic on newspaper
30 x 36 cm
Courtesy of The Modern
Institute/Toby Webster Ltd,
Glasgow

p.6
The Liar's Several Attempts,
2012
Acrylic on pieced newspaper
32 x 45 cm
Courtesy of The Modern
Institute/Toby Webster Ltd,
Glasgow

p.7
Commonwealth Parking, 2012
Acrylic on pieced newspaper
52 x 47 cm
Courtesy of The Modern
Institute/Toby Webster Ltd,
Glasgow

p.9
The Flavours Disappear, 2012
Acrylic on pieced newspaper
43 x 62 cm
Courtesy of The Modern
Institute/Toby Webster Ltd,
Glasgow

p.10
Celebrate Something Else, 2012
Acrylic on pieced newspaper
47 x 61 cm
Courtesy of The Modern
Institute/Toby Webster Ltd,
Glasgow

p.11
First time with a lasso, 2012
Acrylic on newspaper
47 x 40 cm
Courtesy of The Modern
Institute/Toby Webster Ltd,
Glasgow

p.15
Preferred Warning, 2006
Acrylic on pieced newspaper
47 x 63 cm
JoAnn Gonzalez-Hickey
Collection

p.16
Untitled, 2006
Acrylic on pieced newspaper
31 x 31 cm
Collection of John Friedman

p.17
Key or Toffee, 2007
Acrylic on pieced newspaper
43 x 58 cm
Sender Collection, New York

p.19
*Everything**, 2007
Acrylic on pieced newspaper
43 x 28 cm
Private Collection, Ohio

p.20
No Way Near, 2007
Acrylic on pieced newspaper
37 x 45 cm
Private Collection, Nebraska

p.21
Untitled, 2007
Acrylic on pieced newspaper
51 x 42 cm
Courtesy Marianne Boesky
Gallery, New York

p.22
Gunfight of the Mind, 2007
Acrylic on pieced newspaper
84 x 125 cm
Private Collection, Los Angeles

p.25
Too-valued blue, 2007
Acrylic on pieced newspaper
63 x 122 cm
Private Collection, New York

p.26
Untitled, 2007
Acrylic on pieced newspaper
45 x 86 cm
Private Collection, Denver

p.27
Brinkmanship Template, 2007
Acrylic on pieced newspaper
60 x 74 cm
Cobra to Contemporary
Collection of Hugo and
Carla Brown

p.28
Due at six, due at nine, 2007
Acrylic on pieced newspaper
63 x 127 cm
Private Collection, Princeton,
NJ

p.29
Cradle Held Arc, 2007
Acrylic on pieced newspaper
66 x 100 cm
Alastair Cookson Collection,
London

pp.30–31
Ten Miles South of Here, 2008
Acrylic on pieced newspaper
54 x 119 cm
Private Collection, California

pp.32–33 (p.2 detail)
*Jesus Help Me Find My
Property*, 2007
Acrylic on pieced newspaper
76 x 319 cm
Tate Collection. Purchased
with funds provided by the
Nicholas Themans Trust 2009

p.35
Impure Passports, 2007
Acrylic on pieced newspaper
95 x 92 cm
Courtesy of Herald St, London

p.36
Untitled, 2007
Acrylic on pieced newspaper
46 x 17 cm
Courtesy of Herald St, London

p.37
*The family kept changing
shape*, 2008
Acrylic on pieced newspaper
31 x 27 cm
The Pinnell Collection, Dallas

p.38
Slang is Signals, 2007
Acrylic on pieced newspaper
38 x 63 cm
Courtesy of Herald St, London

p.39
Untitled, 2008
Acrylic on pieced newspaper
29 x 45 cm
Courtesy of The Modern
Institute/Toby Webster Ltd,
Glasgow

p.41
Remembered as one, 2008
Acrylic on pieced newspaper
95 x 148 cm
Alastair Cookson Collection,
London

p.47
Detained at the centre, 2008
Acrylic on pieced newspaper
44 x 57 cm
Courtesy of The Modern
Institute/Toby Webster Ltd,
Glasgow

pp.48–49
Untitled, 2008
Acrylic on pieced newspaper
77 x 155 cm
Private Collection, California

p.51
Untitled, 2008
Acrylic on pieced newspaper
61 x 63 cm
Private Collection, Denver

pp.52–53
He Could Have Travelled, 2008
Acrylic on pieced newspaper
53 x 127 cm
Dr Amar Safdar Collection,
Houston

pp.54–55
*With Each Debut,
An Attitude*, 2008
Acrylic on pieced newspaper
47 x 115 cm
Private Collection, New York

p.56
Untitled, 2009
Acrylic on newspaper
47 x 62 cm
Collection of Nancy
and Nate Kacew

p.57
Untitled, 2009
Acrylic on newspaper
27 x 32 cm
Private Collection, New York

p.58
Untitled, 2009
Acrylic paint on newspaper
22 x 31 cm
Courtesy of The Modern
Institute/Toby Webster Ltd,
Glasgow

p.59
You are made of thoughts, 2009
Acrylic on newspaper
36 x 47 cm
Courtesy of Herald St, London

p.61
Untitled, 2009
Acrylic on pieced newspaper
39 x 72 cm
Courtesy of Herald St, London

pp.62–63
Untitled, 2009
Acrylic on pieced newspaper
36 x 181 cm
Courtesy of Herald St, London

p.64
Untitled, 2009
Acrylic on pieced newspaper
31 x 63 cm
Courtesy of The Modern
Institute/Toby Webster Ltd,
Glasgow and Herald St,
London

p.65
Untitled, 2009
Acrylic on newspaper
35 x 23 cm
Collection Hamilton
Corporate Finance

pp.66–67
Era was aware, welfare era flew,
2009
Acrylic on pieced newspaper
72 x 182 cm
Courtesy of Herald St, London

p.68
DNA, slate, metal, sand, 2009
Acrylic on pieced newspaper
47 x 62 cm
Courtesy Shelley Bransten
Perelmuter, San Francisco

p.69
Untitled, 2009
Acrylic on pieced newspaper
33 x 39 cm
Courtesy of The Modern
Institute/Toby Webster Ltd,
Glasgow

pp.70–71
*Dream Re-enactment
Society*, 2009
Acrylic on pieced newspaper
82 x 261 cm
Private Collection, Denver

p.72
Untitled, 2009
Acrylic on newspaper
31 x 15 cm
Courtesy of The Modern
Institute/Toby Webster Ltd,
Glasgow

p.73
Colours at the moment, 2008
Acrylic on pieced newspaper
25 x 17 cm
Courtesy of The Modern
Institute/Toby Webster Ltd,
Glasgow

p.79
Untitled, 2010
Acrylic on pieced newspaper
60 x 130 cm
No Bad Collection, Fife

pp.80–81
Untitled, 2010
Acrylic on pieced newspaper
80 x 182 cm
Courtesy of The Modern
Institute/Toby Webster Ltd,
Glasgow

p.83
Untitled, 2010
Acrylic on pieced newspaper
31 x 27 cm
Courtesy of The Modern
Institute/Toby Webster Ltd,
Glasgow

p.84
Untitled, 2010
Acrylic on pieced newspaper
61 x 57 cm
Kevin and Melinda Johnson
Collection, Woodside, CA

p.85
The Road to Water, 2010
Acrylic on pieced newspaper
58 x 99 cm
Courtesy of Herald St, London

p.87
The Tribute to Inquiry, 2010
Pieced newspaper
17 x 24 cm
Courtesy of Herald St, London

pp.88–89
*Where Everything Lived
For Waiting*, 2010
Acrylic on pieced newspaper
127 x 475 cm
Private Collection, Luanda

p.90 (p.12 detail)
Untitled, 2011
Acrylic on pieced newspaper
70 x 110 cm
Private Collection, Lisbon

p.91
Room by Room, 2011
Acrylic on pieced newspaper
33 x 55 cm
Private Collection, Paris

p.92
*Coping and more than
coping*, 2011
Acrylic on pieced newspaper
26 x 32 cm
Courtesy of The Modern
Institute/Toby Webster Ltd,
Glasgow

p.93
Untitled, 2010
Acrylic on pieced newspaper
62 x 148 cm
Courtesy of Herald St, London

pp.94 (p.42 detail)
Floor Wears Out, 2011
Acrylic on pieced newspaper
65 x 114 cm
Private Collection

pp.96–97 (p.106 detail)
Clues in Formation, 2011
Acrylic on pieced newspaper
119 x 335 cm
Courtesy of The Modern
Institute/Toby Webster Ltd,
Glasgow

p.99 (p.74 detail)
To get is opposite got, 2011
Acrylic on pieced newspaper
166 x 183 cm
Private Collection,
Woodside, CA

p.100
Intimacy Accrued, 2011
Acrylic on newspaper
46 x 62 cm
Courtesy of The Modern
Institute/Toby Webster Ltd,
Glasgow

p.101
The Incremental Stop, 2011
Acrylic on pieced newspaper
46 x 62 cm
Courtesy of The Modern
Institute/Toby Webster Ltd,
Glasgow

p.102
Homes For Sometimes, 2011
Acrylic on pieced newspaper
46 x 62 cm
Courtesy of The Modern
Institute/Toby Webster Ltd,
Glasgow

p.103
Nothing behind Nothing, 2010
Acrylic on pieced newspaper
48 x 66 cm
Courtesy of Herald St, London

p.104
Persistence is, 2010
Acrylic on pieced newspaper
46 x 62 cm
Courtesy of Herald St, London

p.105
*Earlier Less Conventional
Advice*, 2010
Acrylic on pieced newspaper
31 x 56 cm
Courtesy of Herald St, London

pp.108–109
Installation view of
Temperature is here too,
Art Now, Tate Britain,
London, 2009

*Sizes are unframed,
height x width*

ACKNOWLEGEMENTS

Published on the occasion of the exhibition
Tony Swain: Drowned Dust, Sudden Word
19 April – 1 July 2012

The Fruitmarket Gallery, Edinburgh

Exhibition supported by The Fruitmarket Gallery
Programme Patrons: George Morris, Barry Rosen,
Nicky Wilson and Robert Wilson

Published by The Fruitmarket Gallery, Edinburgh
45 Market Street, Edinburgh, EH1 1DF
Tel:+44 (0)131 225 2383
Fax: +44 (0)131 220 3130
info@fruitmarket.co.uk
www.fruitmarket.co.uk

Publication supported by The Modern Institute/
Toby Webster Ltd
14–20 Osborne Street, Glasgow, G1 5QN
Tel: +44 (0)141 248 3711
Fax: +44 (0)141 552 5988
www.themoderninstitute.com

Additional support by Herald St
2 Herald Street, London, E2 6JT
Tel: +44 (0)20 7168 2566
www.heraldst.com

Edited by Fiona Bradley
Designed and typeset by Elizabeth McLean
Assisted by Susan Gladwin

Produced by fandg.com

ISBN 978-1-908612-04-5

Distributed by Art Data
12 Bell Industrial Estate,
50 Cunnington Street, London, W4 5HB
Tel: +44 (0)20 8747 1061
www.artdata.co.uk

Photography by Ruth Clark; Alex Delfanne; Andy Keate;
Tim Nighswander/Imaging4Art.com; © Tony Swain and Tate,
London 2012; Jason Wyche, New York; Chito Yoshida

Cover: *Untitled*, 2011
Acrylic on pieced newspaper
70 x 110 cm
Private Collection, Lisbon

The artist thanks:
The Modern Institute/Toby Webster Ltd, Glasgow;
Herald St, London; Isla Leaver-Yap;
Karla Black; Richard Deal;
The Fruitmarket Gallery, Edinburgh

The Fruitmarket Gallery is a publicly-funded art gallery
of national and international significance, and is Scotland's
leading contemporary art space. The Gallery aims to make
contemporary art accessible without compromising art or
underestimating audiences. Its programme of exhibitions of
Scottish and international artists is world-class and always free.

Publishing is an intrinsic part of The Fruitmarket Gallery's creative
programme, with books published to accompany each exhibition.
Books are conceived as part of the exhibition-making process,
extending the reach and life of each exhibition and offering artists
and curators a second space in which to present their work.

The Fruitmarket Gallery is a company limited by guarantee,
registered in Scotland No. 87888 and registered as
a Scottish Charity No. SC 005576. VAT No. 398 2504 21

Registered Office: 45 Market St., Edinburgh, EH1 1DF

The Fruitmarket Gallery staff:
Director, Fiona Bradley
Deputy Director, Elizabeth McLean
Development Manager, Armida Taylor

Research and Interpretation Manager, Stacy Boldrick;
Programme Assistant, Susan Gladwin; Senior Installation
Technician, Colin MacFarlane; Gallery Manager, Jamie Mitchell;
Commercial Opportunities Manager, Iain Morrison; Learning
Programme Manager, Caitlin Page; Installation Technician,
Simon Shaw; Finance Manager, Celeste Stamenkovic; Press and
Marketing Manager, Louise Warmington; Bookshop Manager,
Matthew Williams; Administrator, Kirsten Wilson;
Exhibitions Organiser, Samantha Woods

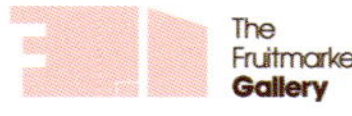
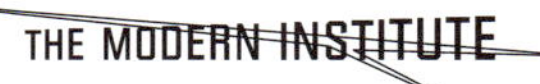
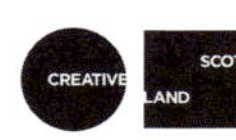

TONY SWAIN

DROWNED DUST, SUDDEN WORD

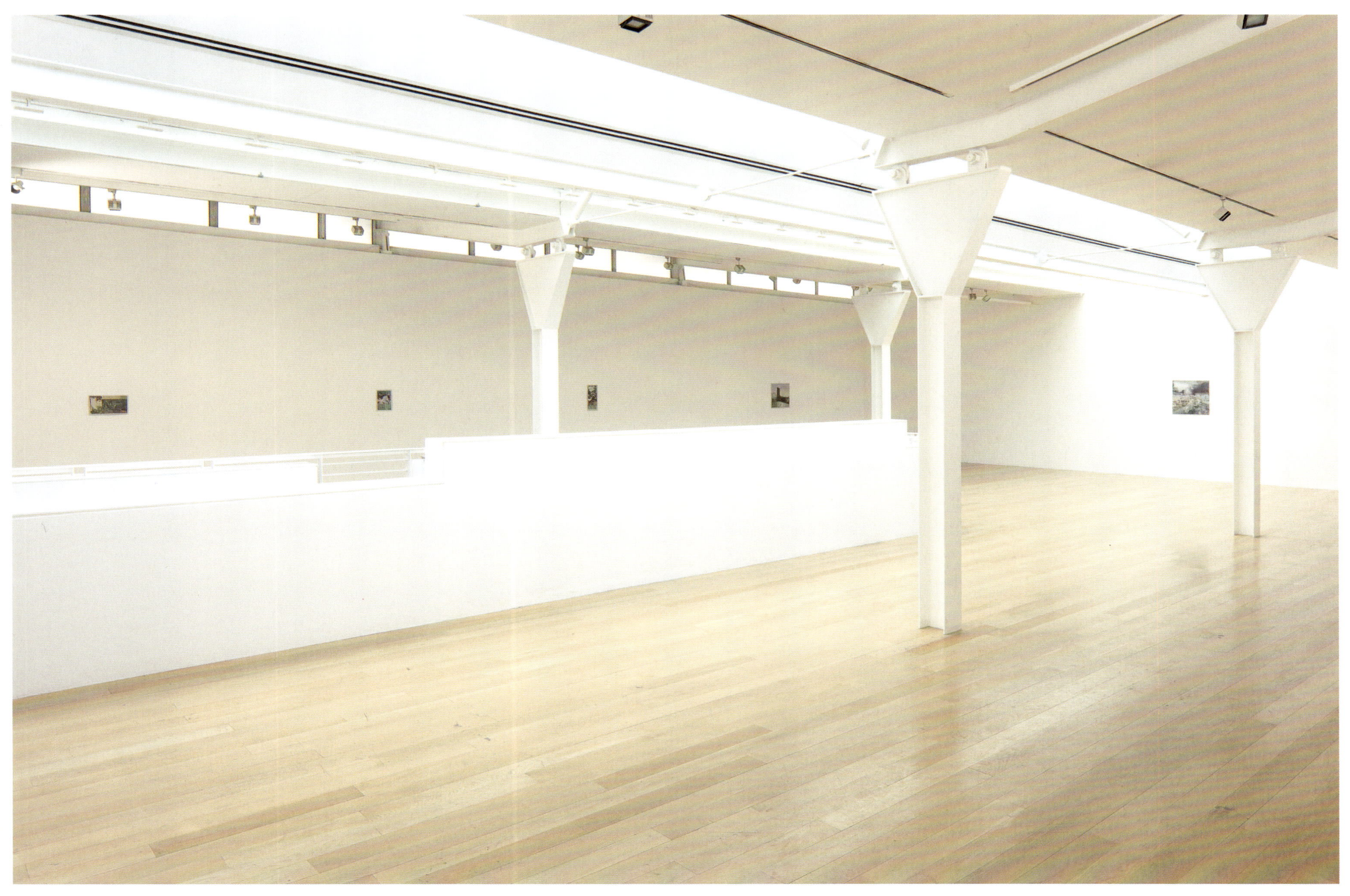

THE FRUITMARKET GALLERY, EDINBURGH

19 APRIL – 8 JULY 2012

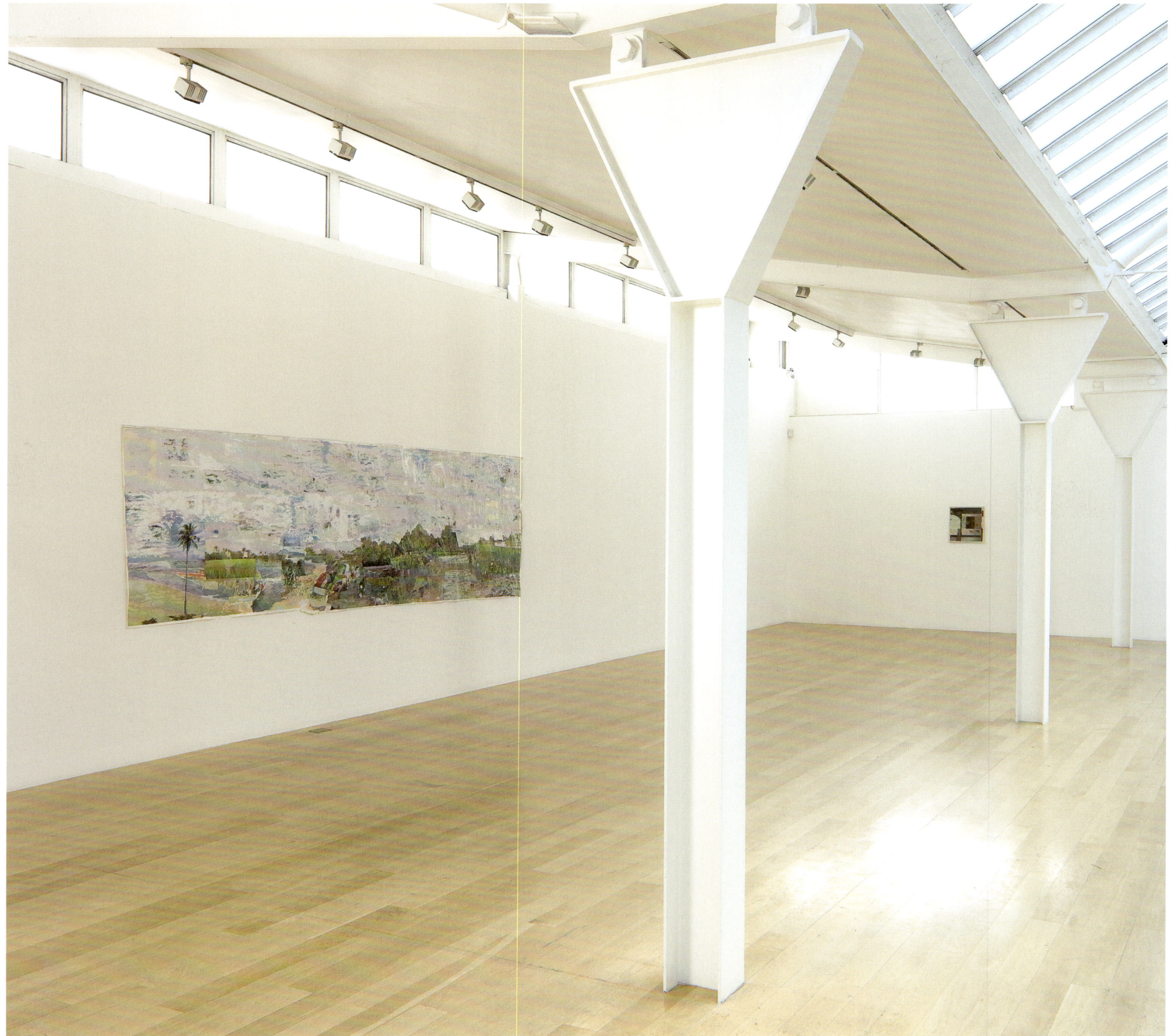

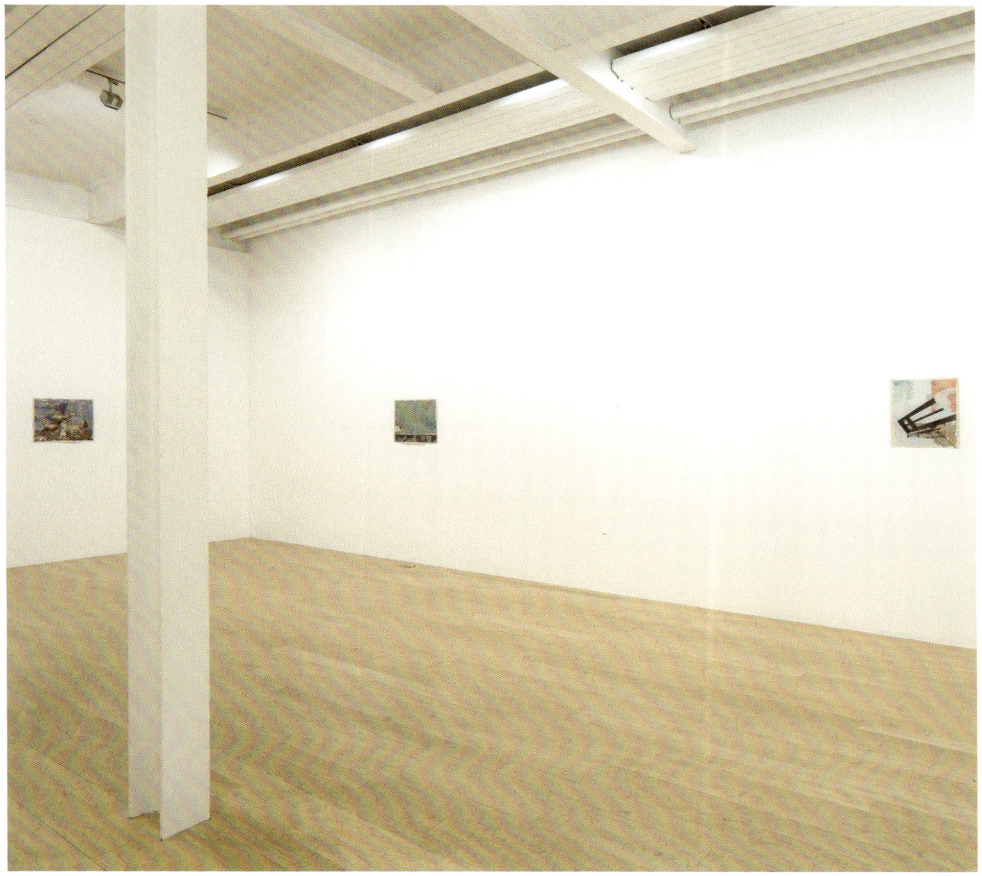

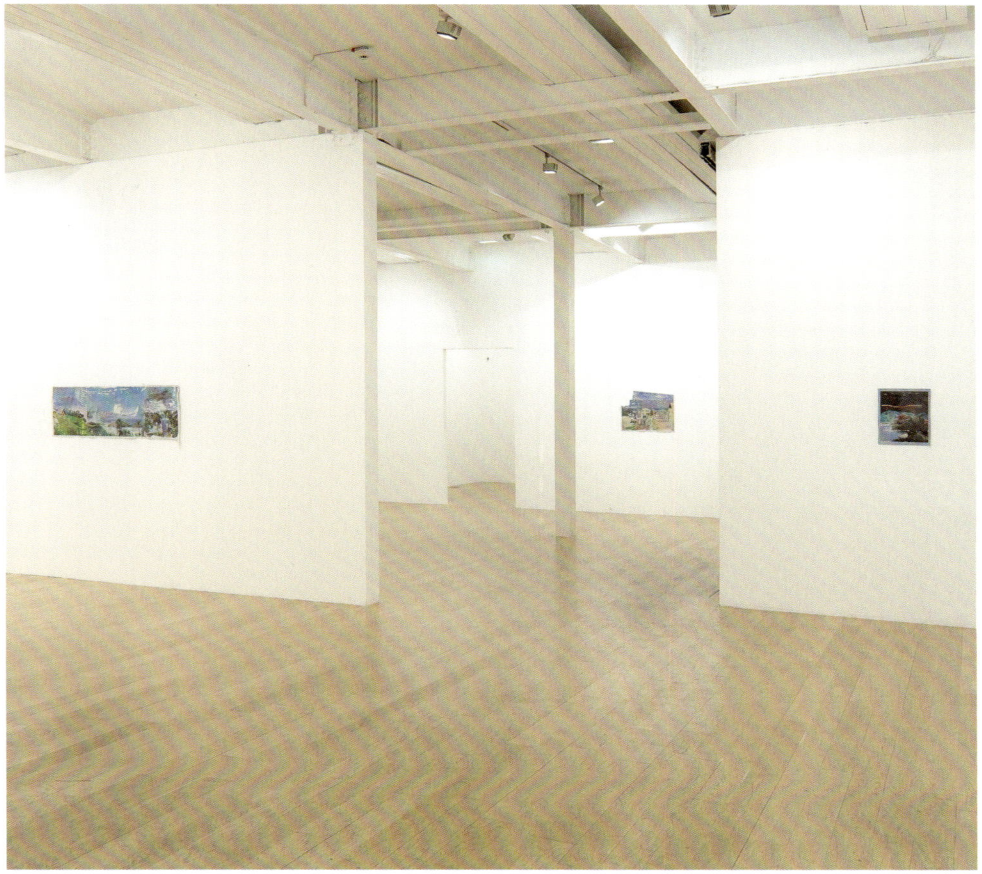

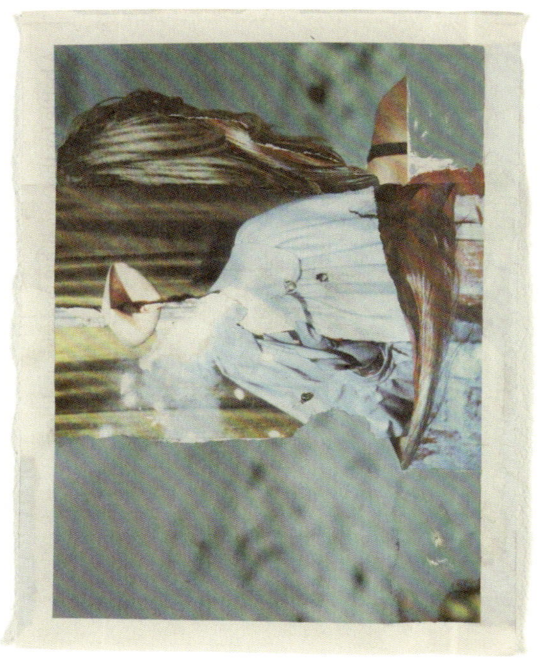

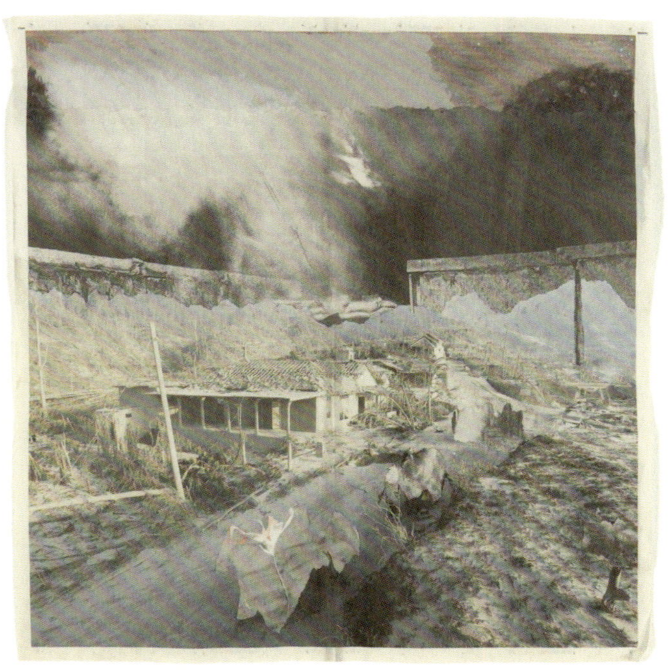

LIST OF WORKS

As universal as revenue
Acrylic on pieced newspaper
59.5 x 71.5 cm

As well
Acrylic on pieced newspaper
132 x 446 cm

Celebrate Something Else
Acrylic on pieced newspaper
47 x 61 cm

Commonwealth Parking
Acrylic on pieced newspaper
52 x 47 cm

First time with a lasso
Acrylic on newspaper
47 x 40 cm

Five die cutting star
Acrylic on pieced newspaper
54.5 x 131 cm

Host Rain, 2012
Acrylic on pieced newspaper
45 x 63 cm

Idle as totems
Acrylic on newspaper
30 x 36 cm

Lifelike surprises
Acrylic on pieced newspaper
46.5 x 61 cm

Next traffic bulletin in seven minutes
Acrylic on pieced newspaper
30 x 21 cm

One dressed as many
Acrylic on pieced newspaper
24 x 40 cm

Providing for
Acrylic on pieced newspaper
54.5 x 62 cm

Put ashore, at his own request
Acrylic on pieced newspaper
41 x 32 cm

Swarm and scold
Acrylic on pieced newspaper
64 x 62 cm

Tariff of fir
Acrylic on pieced newspaper
46 x 23 cm

The Flavours Disappear
Acrylic on pieced newspaper
43 x 62 cm

The Liar's Several Attempts
Acrylic on pieced newspaper
32 x 45 cm

Untitled
Acrylic on pieced newspaper
39.5 x 21.5 cm

Untitled
Acrylic on pieced newspaper
28.5 x 21 cm

Untitled
Acrylic on pieced newspaper
32 x 24 cm

Winter Applies Here
Acrylic on pieced newspaper
37 x 22.5 cm

All works courtesy of
The Modern Institute /
Toby Webster Ltd, Glasgow

Photographs © Ruth Clark

*All works dated 2012
Sizes are unframed,
height x width*

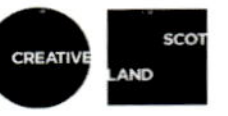